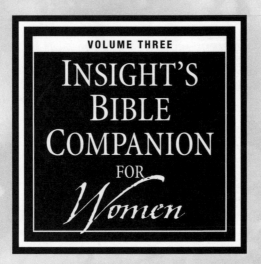

VOLUME THREE

INSIGHT'S BIBLE COMPANION FOR *Women*

INSIGHT FOR LIVING

Insight's Bible Companion for Women, volume 3

Copyright © 2001 by Insight for Living

Published by:
Insight for Living
Post Office Box 269000
Plano, Texas 75026-9000
www.insight.org

ISBN 1-57972-370-5

Notice

Cover Digital Imagery: © Copyright 2001 PhotoDisc, Inc.

Managing Editor: Barb Peil

Designer: Alex Pasieka

Printed in the United States of America

TABLE OF CONTENTS

Introduction

Loving Where You Are

A Heart That's His

AN ENCOURAGING WORD

A Foreword by

Cynthia Swindoll

What do women want? Recent best sellers and movies have tried to explore this topic from every angle, but I think the answer is rather simple. If you're like me, you want to know that your life really matters to God and to others. We need to know that we are valued. Appreciated. Making a difference in our world. Am I right?

I believe this desire stems from the fact that, at the core of our being, we are relational. Women love to relate to others—to other women, to our husbands, to friends, to the members of our family, and to our community of faith and society. *We **love** to connect.*

In keeping with how God has uniquely gifted women, He usually places us in positions of great influence. We may not be the ones in charge, but women have always been that strong yet gentle breeze directing a course.

Consider your home. There's no one who can better influence your child for good than you. At work, your kindness can draw co-workers like a magnet. Your friends lean on you for strength, for advice, for acceptance . . . and for fun. And whether it's obvious or not, your husband considers your opinion the most important one in his world.

Your life, your influence, can have an impact—how broad and how deep are really up to you and God. If I read Deuteronomy 6:5–7 correctly, I understand that He wants us to be very intentional about influencing our world, seizing those everyday opportunities to live what we truly believe. Just listen to these verses:

> *"You shall love the Lord your God with all your heart and with all your soul and with all your might. These words, which I am commanding you today, shall be on your heart. You shall teach them diligently to your sons and shall talk of them when you sit in your house and when you walk by the way and when you lie down and when you rise up."*

The preceding and following verses to this passage make it ever clearer that we are to seize the moments. Just think about seizing every moment—*diligently* seizing every opportunity to teach a principle, give encouragement, and draw upon God's enabling power. That boggles my mind when I contemplate those words as they relate to my experiences this very day.

Back in the fall of 1960, when I was a skinny, scared, and shy young wife with a husband in Dallas Theological Seminary (and long before Bruce Wilkinson wrote the book, *The Prayer of Jabez*), I was preparing an Old Testament Bible study when I came across Jabez's prayer in 1 Chronicles 4:9–10. It was astounding to me, and I longed to know the particulars of God's having granted his request. The Amplified Version reads:

> *Jabez was honorable above his brothers; but his mother named him Jabez (sorrow maker), saying, "Because I bore him in pain." Jabez cried to the God of Israel, saying, Oh that You would bless me and enlarge my border,*

and that Your hand might be with me, and You would
keep me from evil so it might not hurt me!" And God
granted his request.

Sometimes I feel we so focus on God's enlarging our borders that
we forget the other three parts of his prayer: that God would bless
him, that God's hand would be with him, and that God would keep
him from evil so that he would not get hurt. I decided that, rather than
intensely pursuing an understanding of how God had answered Jabez's
prayer, I would try to understand how God answers this prayer when
uttered by *any* of His children. It represents the very foundation of His
role as our Heavenly Father. True, there are many, many aspects to
these requests and our experiencing them in our own personal lives,
but this can indeed be everyone's prayer, and God's granting these
requests can become our own personal adventure.

Jabez's passion was born through pain, but rather than becoming
a victim of his circumstances, he wanted to be a pioneer in the
efforts of enlarging the borders of his existence. He therefore seized
his disadvantage as an opportunity, and he knew that it would
require his setting up a partnership with the living God. God's hand
delivered His signature to the plan and Jabez's actions were handled
with honor—more honor than his brothers who had either experienced or witnessed their mother's pain.

Seizing the opportunities today will prepare you for the mission
and the ministry for which you were created. Much like Esther's
moment, which was correctly stated by her cousin, Mordecai, in
Esther 4:14: "For if you remain silent at this time, relief and deliverance will arise for the Jews from another place and you and your
father's house will perish. And who knows whether you have not

attained royalty for such a time as this?" The many days and years of preparation—sometimes painful years—may result in some unexpected moment, some divine intervention, "for such a time as this."

Seizing the opportunities today will also prepare you to envision a worthy and cherished ambition. For Jabez, it was an enlarged border while God's hand rested upon him. I believe God granted his request because he was more honorable in his thoughts and actions than his brothers. Jabez had learned, as did Micah, that the Lord requires us to do justice, to love kindness, and to walk humbly with our God (Micah 6:8). Jabez had also learned what the Apostle Paul would later learn and express in his letter to the Galatians: "And let us not lose heart and grow weary and faint in acting nobly and doing right, for in due time and at the appointed season we shall reap, if we do not loosen and relax our courage and faint" (Galatians 6:9 AMPLIFIED).

Seizing the opportunities today will reveal your weaknesses and bring you to a greater understanding of God's awesome power and sufficiency. Paul expressed how he had gained this understanding in 2 Corinthians 12:9 AMPLIFIED (emphasis in original):

> But He [the Lord] said to me, My grace—My favor and loving-kindness and mercy—are enough for you, (that is, sufficient against any danger and to enable you to bear the trouble manfully); for My *strength* and *power* are made perfect—*fulfilled and completed and* show themselves most effective—*in (your) weakness*. There, I will all the more gladly glory in my weaknesses and infirmities, that the strength and *power of Christ, the Messiah, may rest*—yes, may pitch a tent (over) and dwell—*upon me!*

In this regard, I just have to give you a quote from F. B. Meyer that says it all:

> My grace is sufficient, *sufficient*, SUFFICIENT for thee! Sufficient when friends forsake, and foes pursue; sufficient to make thee strong against a raging synagogue, or a shower of stones; sufficient for excessive labours of body, and conflicts of soul; sufficient to enable thee to do as much work, and even more, than if the body were perfectly whole—for my strength is made perfect only amid the conditions of mortal weakness.
>
> In estimating the greatness of a man's life-work, it is fair to take into consideration the difficulties under which he has wrought. And how greatly does our appreciation of the Apostle rise when we remember that he was incessantly in pain. Instead, however, of sitting down in despair, and pleading physical infirmity as his excuse for doing nothing, he bravely claimed the grace which waited within call, and did greater work through God's enabling might than he could have done through his own had it been unhindered by his weakness.
>
> Ah, afflicted ones, your disabilities were meant to unite with God's enablings; your weakness to mate His power. Do not sit down before that mistaken marriage, that uncongenial business, that unfortunate partnership, that physical weakness, that hesitancy of speech, that disfigurement of face, as though they must necessarily maim and conquer you. God's grace is at hand—sufficient—and at its best when human weakness is most profound. Appropriate it, and learn that those that wait on God are

stronger in their weakness than the sons of men in their
stoutest health and vigour.
(F.B. Meyer, *Paul: A Servant of Jesus Christ*)

That, in a nutshell, is the Christian life. Through all the very
painful experiences, in season and out of season, in sickness, in
health, when we feel like it and when we don't, when betrayed, when
confused, we burrow through all the layers in search of the truth and
then orchestrate our responses to life's experiences by walking
humbly with God, practicing justice, and loving kindness. In due
time and at the appointed season, we will come to experience our
appointment for "such a time as this."

Never in my wildest dreams would I have envisioned back in 1960,
when I studied Jabez and prayed his prayer, how God would answer
these requests and truly bless Chuck and me through our pastoral
ministries and the ministry of Insight for Living. As a sixteen-year-old
girl, I totally gave my heart without reservations to the ministry of
God's Word and to the Great Commission. Seven months later, after
dating one week, I became engaged (too young!) to a wonderful nine-
teen-year old young man who passionately loved Jesus. God gave
Chuck the gift of pastor-teacher, a gift I do not possess. He gave me the
gift of administration and an off-the-chart vision for reaching the
whole world with God's truth, the only truth that can set men free. Our
borders have indeed included the whole world, and my fears and shy-
ness have been replaced with a greater understanding of the power of
God through unbelievable, I say again, unbelievable circumstances . . .
never predictable and always requiring that we press on through the
valleys and mountains of life. Jabez's expanded borders encompassed
just such valleys and mountains. I'm sure of that.

Soon after the study of Jabez, I studied Philippians 3:10–11 which became for me, my life's verses. I love the Amplified Version:

> *(For my determined purpose is) that I may know Him— that I may progressively become more deeply and intimately acquainted with Him, perceiving and recognizing and understanding (the wonders of His Person) more strongly and more clearly. And that I may in that same way come to know the power outflowing from His resurrection (which it exerts over believers); and that I may so share His sufferings as to be continually transformed (in spirit into His likeness even) to His death, (in the hope) That if possible I may attain to the (spiritual and moral) resurrection (that lifts me) out from among the dead (even while in the body).*

This thought is present in my mind daily: The very power that raised Jesus from the dead is available to us each and every moment of our lives, *every single moment of our lives,* to enable us to be transformed in our spirit into His likeness. Why? So that we may attain to the spiritual and moral resurrection that lifts us out from among the dead—both those unbelievers who are spiritually dead without Christ as well as those believers who are experientially dead, though possessing eternal life. Most in this latter category have no clue about this power. That is a staggering thought. If we were mindful of the power of God through every single moment, through every God-sanctioned, worthy, and cherished ambition, through every sovereign act in our lives, we would live totally different lives. We would live life abundantly. Our borders would be enlarged.

To continue in the tradition of women encouraging women and to make the most of those daily opportunities, Insight for Living brings you *Insight's Bible Companion for Women.* In this unique volume, we focus directly on what women want and need . . . but more importantly, on what *God wants* for us. We hope this resource will provide help in gaining a biblical, practical perspective for all the different roles we play and encouragement in how to deepen our relationship with Christ. It's written completely by women and for women. We've invited some experienced and some seminary-trained women on our staff and women who are mature in ministry to sit with us for a while and share what they have learned about walking with God. I know you'll enjoy these brief visits.

In closing, let me say that my prayer for you is always two-fold:

First, I pray that you will be strengthened and encouraged in your faith as you become a woman of God's Word. I pray that your life will be so saturated with His truth that it will pour out into every area of your influence as you gain a new understanding of God's great and mighty, incredible power that is resident within your person—regardless of what your circumstances have been, what they are now, or what they will be tomorrow. There are no limitations to God's miraculous power as evidenced by His raising His Son, the Lord Jesus Christ, from the dead. Incredible!! Just think about your greatest challenge and measure it against God's awesome power. If God can raise someone from the dead (and He can, and He did), then He certainly can raise you from whatever may be your circumstance. This thought will increase your strength and bring incredible encouragement.

Secondly, I pray that you will become a woman of great vision—indeed, a real vision-caster for a worthy and cherished ambition.

I have learned that the dissemination of God's Word is terribly important to God and that He will use any willing, obedient child to proclaim it and its application to any culture under the sun, but not without many varied and often painful life experiences. Disseminating God's Word through radio involves constant struggles. Nothing ever goes perfectly as planned. I might add that pastoring churches is an equally messy job, and it just never ends.

Part of the key for trekking through the valleys and mountains of your God-given vision is found in verse nine of 1 Chronicles 4 where we learn that through the painful experiences of Jabez's life he was more honorable than his brothers. Don't we wish we knew all that this represented in the lives of his family members? This silence in the text, however, is eloquent because we, too, experience God's answers to this prayer often in silence, unknown and unrecognized by anyone else. It's our own personal adventure — and the vision God casts in our hearts to teach His truth within our homes and families as well as unto the uttermost corners of the globe.

It is my strong desire that all of us will learn to face the many changes and challenges of life with great dreams for what God can and will do through us. The world marvels when it sees women who are confident in their faith and in the Lord, women who are willing to give *all* of their potential to Him.

I like how Chuck describes it, "Vision is spawned by faith, sustained by hope, sparked by imagination, and strengthened by enthusiasm. It is greater than sight, deeper than a dream."

May I ask you — what are you willing to let God do through you that's beyond your wildest dreams?

Life is not a problem to be solved; it is an adventure to be lived. That's the nature of it and has been since the beginning when God set the dangerous stage for this high-stakes drama and called the whole wild enterprise *good*. He rigged the world in such a way that it only works when we embrace *risk* as the theme of our lives, which is to say, only when we live by faith. A man just won't be happy until he's got adventure in his work, in his love and in his spiritual life.
(John Eldredge, *Wild at Heart*)

"Don't ask yourself what the world needs. Ask yourself what makes you come alive, and go do that, because what the world needs is people who have come alive" (Gil Bailie as quoted in *Wild at Heart*).

Ladies, let's come alive and get with it. As always, Chuck and I hope for you the greatest of blessings as you discover that God-sanctioned vision and learn to embrace His miraculous power to get it done. May this volume encourage you in that journey.

Cynthia Swindoll

Cynthia Swindoll
President and Chief Executive Officer
Insight for Living

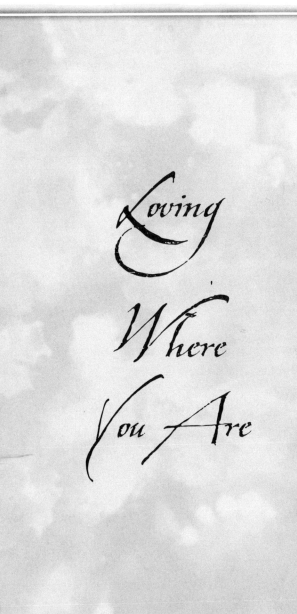

Loving

Where

You Are

LOVE THE LIFE GOD'S GIVEN YOU

by Luci Swindoll

*God can satisfy your wandering search for fulfillment,
and when He does, He will fill you to overflowing.*

My suitcase came off the shelf so fast it would've made your head swim. I was wildly throwing stuff in it when my father walked by the door and asked what I was doing.

"I've had it," I told him flatly. "Mother gives me way too much to do, my homework is too long and boring, my friends don't understand me, and God's too busy to know I'm even down here. I'm running away."

He ambled in, sat down on my bed, and asked if he could help me pack.

Well, s-h-o-o-o-t. I didn't want that. In all my little twelve-year-old fury, I dumped the contents of the bag on the bed and ran outside. I'd show Daddy. I wouldn't run away after all, and he'd just have to put up with my lousy attitude. So there!

Haven't you felt like that a hundred times? *I'm outta here! I don't have to live in this house. You've seen me for the last time. I'm moving. I want out of this family. Forever.* I certainly have. I don't so much anymore, but that's only because I live alone, and if I ran away I'd have to take me with me. (It's like my codependent friend who says that when she gets to the end of her rope, she imagines herself saying to her family, "Get in the car. I'm running away!")

There's no escaping reality, but we all try in a million different ways. Some of us sublimate, others ignore, and many (like me) live in denial. I told my friend Marilyn the other day, "Denial is my reality." She laughed, but there's truth in that, and she knows it. There are numerous times when living in the present is way too difficult, even though I am completely committed to the concept and preach it every chance I get. Like almost everything, it's easier said than done.

My mother used to say, "I'll be so glad when you kids are grown so I can quit making all these lunches." (Don't you know there were many days in our adult years when she thought, "I'd love to make lunch for those kids today.") Family responsibility is what Erma Bombeck referred to as "kids and car pools" and Lily Tomlin called "the world of meatballs and mending." Sameness gets old in a hurry.

In Anne Tyler's wonderful novel, *Ladder of Years*, the daily demands were getting to Delia Grinstead. She felt trapped, used by her husband and children, and tired of the mediocrity of her life. So, while on vacation with her family one summer, she walked away. Casually she meandered down the beach and wandered off. Way off. She found a new town, started a new job, took on a new name, and began a new life. She disappeared from her old life and started over.

Within a matter of months, however, she was back where she started—feeling trapped, used, and mediocre. She changed her circumstances, but her temperament and personality stayed the same; therefore, she did little more than re-create a reality similar to the one she'd supposedly escaped. As a critic said in his review of the book, "It just proves that knowing what you're tired of is not the same as knowing what you want." Delia Grinstead learned that the hard way.

Most of us know what we *don't* want in life, but not so many of us know what we *do* want. And not having what we want, or not wanting what we have, leads to discontentment, if not hopelessness and despair. But I've learned that there are ways around these feelings. We can run away, as Delia did. We can keep accumu-lating—things, people, experiences—trying to find what we *might* want, what's missing. We can learn to pretend that we're completely-satisfied-thank-you. Or . . . we can do the one and only thing that works: turn to God and His Word. It is He who brings about real change in our lives. And how does He do that? By giving us hope.

> *Do the one and only thing that works: turn to God and His word. It is He who gives us hope.*

The person who has a relationship with the God of the universe, through His Son Jesus Christ, can know for sure that his hope is secure. It will not come up short. In fact, Paul tells us in Romans 5:2–5 NIV,

And we rejoice in the hope of the glory of God. Not only so, but we also rejoice in our sufferings, because we know that suffering produces perseverance; perseverance, character; and character, hope. And hope does not disappoint us, because God has poured out his love into our hearts by the Holy Spirit, whom he has given us.

There's a stick-to-itiveness about those words, isn't there? One thing leads to another, then another, and another . . . on and on. Like life. Banking on His infallible Word is the only way I know to deal with my imperfect life in this deteriorating world.

I learned that from my mother. She had a way of making Scripture very practical, and it proved life changing. For example, she held tremendous hope for all three of her children, and her hope came straight from Scripture: "A man's gift maketh room for him, and bringeth him before great men" (Proverbs 18:16 KJV). She wrote that verse on a three-by-five card and taped it above her kitchen sink. "I'm claiming this for my three children," she told my brother one day. While Babe and Orville and I fought over baseballs, household chores, and who ate the last popsicle, Mother was praying about our futures. She was believing God's promise that our various gifts would give us opportunities to minister to people "of importance," as the Living Bible puts it. Her hope for that outcome wasn't in her children (at the moment, we were giving her little hope); her hope was in God's faithfulness to His Word.

Mother also scribbled little comments in hymnbooks, and one day after she died I was leafing though the pages of one and found a hymn she had highlighted years before. I was amazed at verse four of "O Zion, Haste":

Give of thy sons to bear the message glorious;
Give of thy wealth to speed them on their way;
Pour out thy soul for them in prayer victorious;
And all thy spending Jesus will repay.

Mother was proactive about every word of that verse. She had two sons and gave them both to the ministry of Jesus Christ. She supported them with monetary gifts. She prayed for them. Today, both of my brothers are in Christian work, and have been all their adult lives. They minister to everyone, including people "of importance." Scripture promised it. Mother believed it. God brought it to pass. She was serious about hoping in Christ, and her prayer life proved it.

My mother was not a saint. I'm sure there were days when she even wanted to run away. But she learned how to rely on the ever-present grace of God, putting her faith constantly in Him, holding fast to a hope that did not disappoint. I don't know why her children did the very thing she longed for them to do—certainly not because she did everything right all the time. My guess is simply that God answered her prayer. Her example of hoping in Him makes me want to hang on, too, to the goodness of the God who loves me, regardless of the dailiness of life and my own frailties.

But what does that really look like? you might wonder. When your precious teenager is addicted to drugs or your best friend is mad at you or your four-year-old is driving you crazy with her center-stageism, where does hope come in? Let me suggest three practical ways to make it real in your life. I saw these principles incarnated in my mother's life, I've tested them again and again in my own, and I've watched many others bank on them as well.

Accept your reality.

Amy Carmichael said, "In acceptance lieth peace." Solomon advised us to accept what God has given us as a gift: "To enjoy your work and to accept your lot in life—that is indeed a gift from God" (Ecclesiastes 5:19 LB).

During the years I worked for Mobil Oil Corporation, there were numerous times I wanted to leave. Quit. Give it up and find a job that had more personal or spiritual gratification. But I believed God had put me in that environment for a purpose. It wasn't that I didn't like the company or that I didn't have any friends there, but there was a lack in my spirit that seemed constant—a plaguing sense that my daily activities had no eternal value.

I kept asking the Lord to open new doors for me and give me victory over those feelings of discontentment. Finally, after many years, I accepted the fact that God wanted me to work for Mobil and to stay until He moved me for His own good reasons. Peace came to me when I stopped fighting. I stayed with Mobil for thirty years, and I have never regretted it. The financial savings I started there grew to a nest egg that enables me to have a very comfortable retirement (if that time ever comes!). The professional growth and experience of those years have helped me in decision making, goal setting, and general maturing. And friends? To this day, those with whom I worked are among the most precious ones in my life. In fact, two of them travel with me almost everywhere I speak.

I don't know anybody who loves what she does or where she is every minute of the day. But the reality is, we are where we are, and God is doing something right there, whether we see it or not. He wastes nothing. He's growing us up in Himself.

Bring God into your reality.

Bringing God into your reality means being fully present in the moment—not wishing you were somewhere you used to be or somewhere you hope to be. My dear friend Ney Bailey helps me bring God into my reality (and keep Him there) by encouraging me to let my current anxieties be the springboard for praying specifically. In other words, when I'm worried about something, have financial troubles or relationship problems—whatever—I let that troublesome thing be the catalyst for talking to God in straightforward detail. I don't skirt what's bugging me. I don't act like it doesn't exist. I don't go on to other things. Right in the middle of my anxiety, I tell God about it, as if He were my dad.

Ney also says, "Luci, don't edit your prayers." I absolutely love that thought. When a child pulls at his mother's coattail for something he wants, he doesn't stand there thinking, *Now, how should I phrase this . . . let's see. Shall I start with "I want," or is that too forward?* Goodness, no! The kid blurts out his thoughts spontaneously, with total abandon. The sincerity of his heart exposes his deepest desires, petitions, and longings to the parent he loves and trusts. Praying that way to our heavenly Father fosters a bonding that's sweet and comforting.

Make life an adventure.

Would you believe that at the age of sixty-two, I took out a thirty-year loan and bought my first home? Why not? After all, I could still be going strong at ninety-two! Never would I have dreamed that at this time in my life I'd be traipsing all over the country with a bunch of rowdy women, speaking to tens of thousands. What ever happened to retirement? And yet, with the new task God has set before me, He has given me new hope for something for which I pray and wait: trusting Him to turn the world upside down. To be a part of it is just icing on the cake.

You're never too old to start living fully. Ask God for a fresh perspective on your life. Try things you've never tried before. Enlist in a joint project with friends—even with people you don't know. Neighbors. Church buddies. Ask yourself what you want most from life, and go for it. You probably can't get it for yourself, but you can pray about it. My brother Chuck says, "Hope doesn't require a massive chain where heavy links of logic hold it together. A thin wire will do . . . just strong enough to get us through the night until the winds die down." Hope is a heartfelt assurance that our heavenly Father knows what's best for us and never makes a mistake. God says, "Trust me. Remember My Word. Believe . . . and wait."

Of course, our greatest hope lies waiting for us at the end of time, when all God's purposes will be fulfilled. We will go to live with Jesus Christ, who by His grace redeemed us, loved us through our trials, provided joy in the midst of heartache, peace for our troubled hearts, and freedom from a boring lifestyle. We'll be with Him forever—an outrageous reality!

Your mundane, everyday, tiresome life may seem like it isn't going anywhere, but believe me . . . it is. So don't run away and join the circus—as fun as it might be for a while! Take it from Delia Grinstead: "Real life" eventually sets in, and then you need more than wishful thinking to see you through. Thankfully, Christ offers all of us a sustaining hope in the midst of the here and now. Joy and fulfillment are not in another town, another job, another life. They're in your very own heart. Believe it. Clasp His hand and come.

❧ Luci Swindoll ❧

Committed to a life of joy, adventure, and celebration, speaker and author Luci Swindoll has long been provoking smiles and inciting laughter in audiences around the world. "I've found that living a meaningful life is all tied into loving . . . in an intentional, purposeful way," she says. Luci is the only person allowed to call her brother Chuck Swindoll, "Babe."

"The reality is, we are where we are, and God is doing something right there, whether we see it or not."

— *Luci Swindoll*

"It is God who is at work in you, both to will and to work for His good pleasure. Do all things without grumbling or disputing; so that you will prove yourselves to be blameless and innocent, [women] of God above reproach in the midst of a crooked and perverse generation, among whom you appear as lights in the world, holding fast the word of life."

Philippians 2:13–16a

WORTH THE WORK: MARRIAGE FOR A LIFETIME

by Sandra Holt

When you get right down to it, much of life—including marriage—requires that age-old process of working for improvement to gain success.

For a couple of decades I have been working with writers, from junior highers to graduate students and beyond, suggesting ways to improve their writing. I always ask them whether they think writing is a gift or a skill because I want to dispel any notion that there is someone, somewhere, who writes a perfect first draft. In fact, I read to them from the "Acknowledgments" section of Chuck Swindoll's *Grace Awakening*, where he describes his own writing process as "the age-old process most authors still use: blood, sweat, tears, sleepless nights, lengthy stares at blank sheets of paper, unproductive days when everything gets dumped into the trash, and periodic moments when inspiration and insight flow."[1]

After we discuss the fact that some people are more "gifted," if you will, at this skill, we return to the concept that writing is none-theless a skill above all, which fortunately can be learned. Then

---

1. Charles R. Swindoll, *The Grace Awakening* (Dallas, Tex.: Word Publishing, 1990), p. ix.

I share ways they can improve their writing skill, noting that this is homework for a lifetime, that writers who care continually struggle to make their writing better, no matter how many books they've published. When you get right down to it, much of life—including marriage—requires that age-old process of working for improvement to gain success.

Recently, I went to family court with a new friend. Not only did I find the place's name a bit of a misnomer, for it certainly appeared that more anti-family matters were raised and adjudicated than pro-family matters, but I was dumbfounded when I heard the judge say, "Granted. You now have a restraining order: He must stay fifty feet from you at church."

Questions began sloshing about in my head: What did it take to get to this point? How could two people who once loved each other hurt each other like this?

I am in no way saying that there should never be a divorce in the church. However, when the divorce rate within the church walls is as great as it is outside, we would do well to stop long enough to ask, What difference does it make to an individual marriage that one or both partners is a Christian? How should my Christianity influence my marriage?

Family court left me thinking that marriage counselors really would do well to encourage their counselees to observe such proceedings, to impress upon them what sadness people—yes, even Christians—visit on each other when they choose to quit working on their marriage.

Practicality is probably the hallmark of my approach to these matters. Having watched my own parents tromp through six divorces, I've seen firsthand that not much is gained by divorce, especially because I know they lived out their days pining for what they could have had if they made their marriage work, namely loving companionship.

The more I thought about how Christians might stave off a stake in family court, the more I realized that marriage is as much a skill as writing. There are no "gifted" marriages that I know of— marriages where the participants don't have to work at keeping the thing alive, keeping it vibrant, and, for some, just keeping it at all. I tell writers that they don't write and then rewrite the blood, sweat, and tears stuff because they are bad writers but because working hard to get it right is the nature of writing. Likewise, working hard to get it right is also the nature of marriage maintenance.

> *There are no "gifted" marriages that I know of—marriages where the participants don't have to work at keeping the thing alive, keeping it vibrant, and, for some, just keeping it at all.*

Marriage-as-a-skill appears first in Titus 2:3–4, where older women are admonished to teach younger women how to love their husbands. If how to love your husband is supposed to be taught, then we can assume the skill can be learned, practiced, and improved. The passage goes on to talk about what kinds of things should be taught, including how to be kind and good. In my own experience and observations, I've found the following reflections to be helpful as well . . .

Perfection. There are no perfect marriages, so you can give that one a rest. Think about it: If the marriage was perfect and he was perfect, where would you fit? A pretty good marriage is a worthy goal.

Projects. Husbands were never meant to be home-improvement projects—unless, of course, you've been notified that the Holy Spirit has taken the day off. Years ago, an old proprietor in a beauty salon displayed an even older sign that read, "Quit trying to make people over into your own image. You know—and God knows—that one of you is enough." Give your guy a break. Let him be who he is.

Career. How about making marriage your career? Gary Habermas has said that materialism is a blight on Christianity. Could materialism also be a blight on marriage? Recently a successful, young, female attorney I know suggested that perhaps women should listen to that nagging little voice in their head that calls them to dump the career and keep the marriage.

The company you keep. Think about the people in your life—friends, relatives, coworkers. Now think about which of those people most support your marriage. Plan to spend more time with them and less time with those who would undermine it, either by design or default. Don't keep company with bitter or discontented women, or before long you'll be tempted to join their ranks.

The Golden Rule. There are few marital issues that would not be positively affected by a "do unto others what you would have them do unto you" approach. How would you love your husband to listen to you recount your day, to champion you in public, to resolve your misunderstandings? Give him a model to follow in how you treat him.

Humor. Apply generously. It's a miracle worker in itself.

Ebenezer. We humans are a forgetful lot, are we not? That's why Samuel made a stone monument he called "Ebenezer"—to remind the Israelites what God had done for them (1 Samuel 7:12). We wives, being human, sometimes forget too. Why not make a list of all the good qualities that drew you to choose that man of yours in the first place, and then add to it all the good things he has done for you? Call it your "Ebenezer List," and put it where you'll read it often.

Allocation of time and energy. Go beyond the mere making of to-do lists, specifically because to-do lists only get the urgent things done, not necessarily the things that matter most. Ponder the important—make a list of what matters most to you, based on biblical principles. Then make sure what's on your daily calendar reflects what you came up with. For instance, if time with your husband is important, write your husband into your schedule rather than dedicating all your energy to the lesser matters that insist on calling themselves "urgent."

Even the state of California has come to realize that there is just so much energy to go around and has had to prioritize how electrical energy is going to be used. Just today I relinquished our 30+-year-old Philco refrigerator that we had in the garage to chill drinks. The Edison Company's been after me for years to get rid of it because it uses too much electricity—energy that could be better used to light, say, a hospital. We all face the same challenge—our very own energy crisis. We have a finite amount of energy that must be used wisely.

Sex. It's not just for procreation anymore, ladies. I knew we were in big trouble when I heard that sweet, young thing at a marriage conference stand up and tell all assembled there that she and her husband only had time for sex once a month. So, put it on your daily activity list if you need to.

Though this list may be too overwhelming to implement at one time, hopefully you'll find one area to get started on as you work to improve your husband-loving skills. Remember, just like in writing, there are no perfect first drafts in marriage, it takes a lot of hard work to get it right, and it's homework for a lifetime. Enjoy!

❖ *Sandra Holt* ❖

*S*andra Holt has taught full-time on the college level for many years. Now she teaches part-time and works with her husband in their small business, where "the pay is better and staff meetings are great." She is thankful that she waited through the wintry seasons of her marriage in order to see the springtime again. She and her husband will soon celebrate their thirty-seventh anniversary.

Be good wives to your husbands, responsive to their needs. There are husbands who, indifferent as they are to any words about God, will be captivated by your life of holy beauty. What matters is not your outer appearance—the styling of your hair, the jewelry you wear, the cut of your clothes—but your inner disposition.

Cultivate inner beauty, the gentle, gracious kind that God delights in. The holy women of old were beautiful before God that way, and were good, loyal wives to their husbands. Sarah, for instance, taking care of Abraham, would address him as "my dear husband." You'll be true daughters of Sarah if you do the same, unanxious and unintimidated.

1 Peter 3:1–2 (THE MESSAGE)

So, You're Married to the Pastor?

by Michele Calvert

*Partnering in ministry offers both blessings and trials.
Explore the secret to contentment in life and
ministry in one of the Bible's favorite passages.*

You have a privileged position as a partner in your husband's ministry. You're able to see firsthand how God is working in your own life and in the lives of others. Since only three things last forever— God, His Word, and people—He is using you and your husband to influence people for eternity. What a benefit for full-time ministry!

But let's face it. Full-time ministry has its stresses, too. Your husband's schedule keeps him many evenings away from home. And on that rare night when everyone's home, the unexpected phone call will tear your husband away to help someone in their time of need.

And then there's the other stresses. Your own schedule keeps you running. Perhaps the paycheck is not up to marketplace standards. People often criticize rather than encourage. They can point out problems rather than seek solutions. God may allow circumstances to mature you because you are in leadership. How do you handle these stresses and your own unique ones?

Rather than complain or become anxious, let's run to Philippians 4:1–13, where Paul listed several practical things we can do to wisely handle our lives in ministry.

Stand firm in the Lord (v. 1)

Previously, in chapter 3 of Philippians, we're reminded that our citizenship is in heaven. Our Savior will return victorious. We will be transformed by His power. Because of these things, we can stand firm in the Lord. But Ephesians 6:12–13 reminds us, "Our struggle is not against flesh and blood, but against the rulers, against the powers, against the world forces of this darkness, against the spiritual forces of wickedness in the heavenly places. Therefore, take up the full armor of God, so that you will be able to resist in the evil day, and having done everything, to stand firm." Your circumstances are more than you think. Your struggle is not against people, though sometimes it appears that way. Remember that a bigger battle, a spiritual one, is raging around you.

You are trying to defeat the enemy by adding to God's army (evangelism) and by increasing the present army's dependence and strength in the Lord (discipleship). God is rescuing those in the "domain of darkness" and transferring them to the kingdom of His beloved Son (Colossians 1:13). Your responsibility is to stand firm in His strength, not your own. Depend on Him. He is the powerful One; you only need be available.

Live in harmony in the Lord (v. 2)

But being available to be used in people's lives means you have to be *involved* in people's lives. That's not always an easy or enjoyable task! Paul urged Euodia and Syntyche, who were Christians and fellow workers with Paul, to live in harmony in the Lord. People have their differences, but we're not called to live in unison—we're called to live in tune with each other. Expect differences, then work them out kindly and lovingly (see Ephesians 4:25–32).

Rejoice in the Lord (v. 4)

Paul said, "Rejoice in the Lord always; again I will say, rejoice!" *Always* and *again I will say*—do you get the impression Paul wanted us to rejoice? We tend to look at the negative and then extrapolate the situation to its worst conclusion. That seems to be human nature. But Paul's command is to rejoice—not in circumstances, but in the Lord. We can always rejoice about Jesus and His love and power, even if our circumstances aren't joyful in themselves.

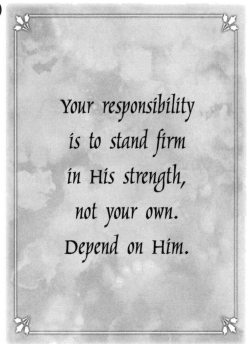

Your responsibility is to stand firm in His strength, not your own. Depend on Him.

Let your gentle spirit be known to all men (v. 5)

We need to rejoice in the Lord even when our circumstances aren't joyful so that our responses to others will be kind and gentle.

Whether it's the grocery check-out clerk, the lady at the back of the church (and you know who she is), or our families, people see God through us. We need to depend on Him and rejoice in Him so that we are able to be kind and gentle to those we need and those who need us.

Be anxious for nothing (v. 6)

What if your circumstances are trying? What should you do? Worry is not the answer! We all want the peace of God in our lives regardless of circumstances. God says the way to have that peace is not to worry but to talk to Him about it. Talk to Him about specific issues with a thankful heart. You may not have the newest furniture. Your kids may have health problems. You may be lonely. People may not be happy about decisions you or your husband have made. How are you going to respond? Are you going to worry or talk with God?

Dwell on these things (v. 8)

What are you going to think about? Paul asked us not to dwell on negative, false, or bitter things. If you're thinking negatively about your-self or your husband or a ministry situation, mentally go through a list of what is true, honorable, right, pure, lovely, of good repute, excellent, and worthy of praise in that situation. Then sit down and write out that list. When the negative comes up, think about the positive.

In the bigger picture, have you taken time lately to think about what's important in your life? What are your priorities? Sit down and write out the stresses and blessings in your unique situation. Your list of blessings is a Philippians 4:8 list to ponder. Thank God for them and dwell on those things.

Practice these things (v. 9)

The command in verse 8 was about those things that occupy your thinking. This last command is about those things that occupy your actions. You want God to be with you, don't you, in every situation and circumstance? Of course you do. Paul said that if we modeled our lives after God's desires, the God of peace would be with us.

Paul said to practice what he preached and modeled. Then he gave a very practical example in the next verses. He talked about contentment—material, financial contentment: "I have learned to be content in whatever circumstances I am" (v. 11). Paul was in prison at the time he wrote this letter. While most of us aren't in that extreme circumstance, Paul wanted us to be content whether in humble means or prosperity: "In any and every circumstance I have learned the secret of being filled and going hungry, both of having abundance and suffering need. I can do all things through Him who strengthens me" (vv. 12b–13). What's in your house doesn't matter; your heart makes the home. *Contentment.* How are you doing in this area?

Full-time ministry has blessings and stresses, just like other jobs. The schedule gives both the blessing of flexibility and the stress of evenings away or quick trips to the hospital. Maybe your paycheck is less than a marketplace paycheck. Maybe your congregation has unrealistic expectations of you. If communication is the problem, kindly fix it. If you can't say no, ask God to show you what one area of ministry He wants you to concentrate on for this time. Then say "no" for now to those other things. Choose to be content where you are. That's not status quo; that's peace with Jesus because you stand firm in Him, living in harmony with others, not worrying, thinking on good things, and living a contented, godly life . . . while making an impact for eternity. What a privileged position!

⋙ Michele Calvert ⋘

*M*ichele met her husband Chris while they were both students at Dallas Theological Seminary. She says, "Every Christian should be a full-time Christian, but it has been a privilege to be in full-time vocational ministry with Chris for the last eight years." The Calverts minister at Memorial Bible Church in Yakima, Washington.

A Woman's Daily Life in Jesus' Day

Proverbs isn't kidding when it says that the virtuous woman works hard. "She rises while it is still night" (31:15) and "she does not eat the bread of idleness" (v. 27). A good wife and mother of Jesus' day worked long hours in maintaining her home.

Food preparation monopolized most of her day. Her family's breakfast was usually eaten on the run: a handful of nuts, raisins, some bread or olives, and possibly a handful of parched grain served them for lunch. But it was the preparation of the evening meal of cooked stew, occasionally with meat and a side dish of vegetables, fruit, and fresh bread that consumed most of her time.

Women needed to draw fresh water from the local well or spring at least twice a day, early in the morning and the early evening, usually to avoid the heat. Often, the women would combine this chore with a social event. Together at the well, the women of the town would exchange news, gossip, and stories while they drew their families' water.

Women in Jesus' day may have also chosen to be:

- midwives
- domestic servants
- fabric merchants
- weavers
- fullers (ancient "dry cleaner")
- tentmakers
- shepherdesses
- cooks
- cheese makers
- food merchants
- innkeepers
- prophesiers
- professional wailers (mourner)

BEYOND EXPECTATIONS: ENJOYING THE SINGLE LIFE

by Barb Peil

*Going through life solo?
Do it God's way!*

I'm doing something this month that I never expected to do as a single woman. I am buying a house. For me, buying a house has always been the epitome of "settling down"—reserved for that time shortly after you get married, after scrimping and saving, after deciding where you want to grow roots. So, while I have been still single, buying a home was out of the question.

But then I realized what was so tweaked in that assumption: *Still single*. Presupposing *someday* married, and, buried a little deeper, *should have been married by now*. I shouldn't buy a home because that expectation was reserved for married folks? How silly.

Now, I don't know if I will or won't be married someday—that belongs to another discussion. But, to be certain, I fling wide the door to problems when I base my decisions on *should*s *or should not*s. Need a few examples? By the time you're 30 . . . or 40 . . . or 50, you *should* be (you fill in the blank).

The expectations are as varied as our families, our histories, and our dreams. I have one friend who for years felt like a total failure because her family expected her to get married at 25, which she did, and to have three babies at two-year intervals, which she didn't. God had other plans. He didn't allow her to conceive for five years. Imagine the heartache she felt at family gatherings when good-hearted but much-too-verbal aunts reminded her of her biological clock.

But I guess I don't have to remind you of that pain, do I? Single women seem to be in the direct firing line of comments like, "A nice girl like you should have no trouble finding a man," or unsolicited advice about where you should go or what you should do to find those nice men. Unfortunately, the Christian community doesn't do very well here, either. Separating single adults out of the congregation in order to help them match up or share in common woes does little to encourage a mature perspective on how God directs our lives — single or married.

I have an idea. Let's take all the "should be's" surrounding our single status and put them out with the trash. In their place, let's build our homes, our perspectives and attitudes, and, yes, even our expectations on our faith in God's character and His personal plan for our lives. Someone else's expectations for your life or even your own dreams pale in comparison to God's plans for you when you depend on Him to direct your path. When we surrender the blueprint of our lives to Him, He can build a life for us nothing short of that "abundantly beyond all that we ask or think" (Ephesians 3:20). In other words, He's waiting for us to say to Him, "Here I am, Lord. Surprise me."

In my new home, I'm going to have a garden. I've planned it all out in my mind — some fruit trees here and flowers there. I've decided to do this not because I especially love to garden, but because I want the constant reminder that God is growing something beautiful in my life too. Something beyond my expectations. Like a good gardener, I live expectantly. I'd like to offer you a few "cuttings" from my garden that, if you choose, you can plant in your own.

1. Cultivate hope.

I won't deny it—being single sometimes has its downside. But God calls you and me to persevere in this struggle. Romans 5 says that in this perseverance, He produces His character in us. And that character gives us hope. And that hope never disappoints, "because God has poured out his love into our hearts by the Holy Spirit, whom he has given us" (vv. 3–5 NIV). When you believe against all hope (Romans 4:18) that God

> *Contentment doesn't mean complacency. It doesn't mean you've given up hope that God will grant your wildest dreams. It just means you've decided to live by faith.*

will be faithful to the abundant life He has promised, then you are living expectantly . . . cultivating hope.

2. Plant peace.

The seed you sow is the plant you get. Plant tomatoes and you get tomatoes . . . not zucchini or eggplant. As a single woman, choose very carefully the thoughts that you let root in your mind. They will determine what grows. Isaiah 26:3 promises God will give you His peace, His *shalom,* if you will lean your mind not on yourself, but on Him—if you will trust Him in every circumstance. If you plant *shalom,* you get *shalom.*

So, in what circumstance do you need peace today? Facing a frightening situation? Lean on Him. Feeling panicked, not knowing what you should do? Trust Him with it. Worried about your job, someone you love, or a situation outside your control? Give it to God and then refuse to let its roots burrow in your mind. Instead, plant peace.

3. Guard your heart's desires with wisdom.

The heart is tricky. Perhaps that's why Proverbs 4:23 says we are to "watch over it with all diligence." Too many broken, wounded hearts belong to women who give it away too easily. Yet, perhaps by default, many women have also built walls around their hearts, making them impervious, safe, and empty.

Unfortunately, I've done both and have learned that I can't always trust my heart. Instead, I'm learning to trust the Lord of my heart to give me wisdom in my relationships and protect me from harm. When someone knocks on my heart's door, I let Him answer it.

4. Leave the growing to God.

Just as a gardener can't force rain or growth, you can't make your single status "work" on your own. God is aware of exactly what you need as a woman, even a single woman. He knows you need financial security, as well as a sense of significance. He understands your longing for emotional and physical intimacy that can only be satisfied by a godly husband. Understanding that He is good and that He is faithful, release these needs to Him and be content. (You knew that word would show up somewhere, didn't you?!)

Contentment doesn't mean complacency. It doesn't mean you've given up hope that God will grant your wildest dreams. It just means you've decided to live by faith—accepting from God's hand what He has for you *today* and offering Him your dreams about tomorrow. Knowing He is involved, today becomes enough.

5. Celebrate your single-best opportunities.

Invest your time. More than your married friends, you have more discretionary time. How are you spending it? Do you spend too much time alone? Rather than pursuing private hobbies or protecting yourself, think about how you can invest that time and energy in cultivating relationships. Or perhaps you spend *too little* time alone. You hate going home to an empty apartment so you are forever with people. Tell the Lord about this sadness or fear. Invite Him along with you wherever you go, whether that be to a restaurant, to the park, to the mall, or on a walk. Make your time alone, time alone *with Him*.

Live unselfishly. You may have no one to think about in your daily routine other than yourself. This freedom could easily default to selfishness. What could you adjust or include in your schedule that is intentionally for someone else's benefit? Open your life, your home, your kitchen to others. Who said hospitality is practiced only by married folks? Instead of expecting others to include you in their homes or holidays, be the first to open your heart and home.

Take a chance. As a single, you may have more chances for adventure. As Luci Swindoll's life and book title so clearly says, your bed may be narrow, but sister, your world can be oh, so wide! Next time you hear about an opportunity to do something out of your comfort zone, say yes! Risk a little! What may not seem so important now could be the most significant experience of your life.

It's exciting to think that a month from now, I will be living in my first home. But I'm even more thrilled about my expectations for the far future. Why? Because contrary to all the *should*s surrounding my single status, my expectations are based on my trust in God's promise to do abundantly above what I could ask or think, according to His power at work within me (Ephesians 3:20).

Until then, you can find me in the garden — cultivating some hope, planting a little peace, and growing in wisdom. You can join me there or plant your own garden. I love what Charles Spurgeon says — we are "not a wilderness but a *garden of the Lord*: walled by grace, planted according to a divine plan, tended by love, weeded by heavenly discipline and constantly protected by divine power."

You grow, girl.

⋙ Barb Peil ⋘

"*A*ll my life, I've been surrounded by wonderful, godly, single women who have led large lives. Full. Complete. Significant. God has been good to give me such models. Now it's my turn!" Barb Peil, IFL's managing editor, was among the first women graduates of Dallas Theological Seminary and is thrilled at the opportunity to communicate God's grace. A recent California transplant, Barb now makes her home in McKinney, Texas.

How Can I Please God?

Ever wonder what God's expectations are of you? Would you like to know how to please Him? You'll find His requirements easier to know because they're written in His Word. And perhaps easier to do, since what He requires of us He enables us to do through the power of His Spirit. The list is neither exhaustive nor one you can ever check off as completed. Instead, it's a list of character-defining decisions to continue to make throughout your lifetime.

How you can please God? Here is how to begin . . .

1. *Love Him.* (Matthew 22:36–37)
   Jesus told us that loving God is the place to begin. Under this umbrella of love, you are able to do the following . . .

2. *Trust Him.* (Proverbs 3:5–6; Hebrews 11:1)
   Like a daughter of a loving parent, you can depend on God to provide all that you need. Believe He has your best at heart.

3. *Know and obey His Word.* (Psalm 119; 2 Timothy 3:14–17)
   A treasure waiting to be discovered! God's Word holds the riches of your relationship with your Father. It comforts, guides, and instructs you on what pleases God.

4. *Keep short accounts with Him and others.* (1 John 1:9; James 5:16) God calls you to a pure life—a holy life that reflects His character. When you fall short of the life God calls you to live, be quick to confess your sin to Him. Your Father waits to span the distance that your sin has caused. Humility and confession are also crucial in your other relationships.

5. *Be others-oriented—loving, kind, and patient as you serve others.* (Ephesians 4:31–32; Colossians 3:12–14; Philippians 2:3–4) Follow Jesus' model as you consider others' needs as priorities.

Continued on next page

How Can I Please God?

Continued from previous page

6. **Cultivate a humble and grateful spirit.** (Colossians 3:15–17)
   What's the source of a humble and grateful spirit? Scripture says it's letting God's Word dwell in you. When you do, you'll see yourself and your circumstances from an entirely different perspective.

7. **Pray in all circumstances.** (1 Thessalonians 5:17)
   Unceasingly. Always in the back of your mind. Always aware that Your Father is a breath away—that's how God desires you to talk with Him.

8. **Be sensitive to the Spirit's influence.** (Hebrews 4:7)
   Do you sense the need to act or respond to Scripture? It may be God's Spirit. Act on it today!

9. **Worship Him.** (Romans 12:1)
   Worship includes, but is not limited to, a church service. It is a service of your life—ascribing to God the praise and adoration He deserves.

10. **Give generously toward His work with time, money, and effort.** (2 Corinthians 9:7)
    Did you know that the word *gift* can also be translated *grace*? When you give, you extend grace to the body of Christ.

11. **Speak kindly.** (Psalm 141:3; Proverbs 31:26; James 3:1–5)
    It sounds like such a simple thing, but oh, how difficult it is to honor one another in our speech. Set a guard over your lips.

12. **See life in terms of eternity.** (Psalm 90:12)
    Worried about something today? Keep it in perspective. You are bound for eternity—focus your priorities there.

HOLD AND RELEASE: LOVING AND SURRENDERING YOUR CHILDREN TO GOD

by Michele Calvert

Follow the Bible's lead in learning how to entrust your children to God's plan and care.

Some days when you think of your child, you think, *What a precious treasure!* Other times you think, *I'm done! No more whining, no more messes, no more discipline problems!*

But the truth is, you're never really done. God has entrusted a life to your care, and that care is *for* life. True, the responsibility for that life is released a piece at a time, and your child is ultimately responsible to God for himself, but as a parent, you have a great opportunity to help him learn to glorify God. One of our greatest callings as a parent is to rear our children so they will love and serve God all the days of their lives.

As we begin to explore a biblical model for that godly task, remember this: All you can do is your best, and you're guaranteed that won't be perfection. You're going to make mistakes, no doubt about it. But God wants to use you and your children in incredible ways if you will trust Him and do what He says.

Hannah's story in 1 Samuel 1 and 2 teaches us four invaluable lessons about motherhood. Now, Hannah wasn't a mom in the beginning of her story—quite the opposite. Her husband, Elkanah, had two wives, Hannah and Peninnah. Peninnah had children; Hannah didn't. In Hannah's culture, children were a sign of God's blessing—obey God, and blessings shall overtake you (Deuteronomy 28:1–4, 11). So, no children, no blessing. Everyone knew it.

The holidays were particularly difficult for Hannah. Once a year, they went to the temple at Shiloh to offer sacrifices. Everyone went—Peninnah and her pack of kids, Elkanah . . . and Hannah. People watched and whispered. Elkanah tried to show his love for Hannah by treating her specially and giving her a double portion of meat at the festival, but Hannah just couldn't eat.

Then, one year when Hannah went to the tabernacle, things changed. Hannah poured out everything before the Lord, and she asked for something specific: a son. She vowed that if she were blessed with a son, she would give him back to the Lord for all the days of his life. After she prayed, Eli the priest spoke with her and said, "Go in peace; and may the God of Israel grant your petition that you have asked of Him" (1 Samuel 1:17). Go in peace she did.

Hannah released the dream of having a child to God. Sound familiar? We'll need to release our children to God many times in our lives: the first day of kindergarten or the first day of college, the day they leave to be a missionary in South America or the day they leave for prison. The child is ultimately responsible to God for his actions, good and bad. And God is a great God; He will guide them as they seek Him. We can have a great impact on our children if we first release them—entrust them—to God.

Hannah trusted God. And when God did bring Samuel into her life, she showed her love for God by obeying Him and keeping her vow (1 Samuel 1:22–28). After Samuel was weaned, Hannah took him to the house of the Lord at Shiloh, and she released him to the Lord's care. She kept her promise, but she always loved her son. Every year when they went up to Shiloh, she took a coat she had made for Samuel. Imagine what that felt like for Hannah—happy tears of pride upon seeing her son, and sad tears of peace upon leaving him. What made her able to release? As we look at her life, four things stand out.

Give your children to the Lord in your heart—acknowledge that they are His precious gifts entrusted to you for a short while.

- **Hannah knew God intimately.** She couldn't pass on something she didn't have herself, and we can't either. We must cultivate our own relationship with God through Jesus Christ. As a mom with young children, just reading the Bible each day and praying with your children at bedtime may be all you can do. God knows that. Each season has its own look. Be honest with Him. He knows already, but you need to tell Him how you see it and let Him remind you of how it really is.

- **Hannah prayed.** She prayed before and after Samuel was born, both alone and in his company (1 Samuel 1:10–12; 2:1–10). A key to intimacy with God is prayer, talking with Him. In the stresses of life, pray quick prayers, but make time to have nice long visits with Him too.

- **Hannah kept her promises.** Keeping your promises with God is obviously important, but keeping your promises with your children is just as important. Things come up that you can't control. Be honest with your children and apologize if necessary. And be realistic in your promises. If you're not sure you'll be able to follow through, don't promise . . . even in the little things.

- **Hannah showed her love.** Every year, she made a coat for Samuel and took it to him. You show your love in many ways, but make sure you tell them. Give them lots of hugs, and say "I love you!" as often as you can. You take care of their clothes and food, but you can also do things that say, "You're special, and I love you"—a card in the mail, flowers or balloons, an ornament for Christmas, a special book or picture, their favorite treat, or something they've been wanting that you can give them for no particular reason.

As moms, what do we want for our children? We want them to love God with all their hearts and to walk with Him all of their days. Hannah's son Samuel did this. Read the rest of 1 Samuel. In his later years, Samuel told the children of Israel that he would teach them the good and right way. He warned them to "fear the Lord and serve Him in truth with all your heart; for consider what great things He has done for you" (1 Samuel 12:24).

So, how are you doing, Mom? Are you teaching your children

those things that are good and right, whether they are children in your home or adult children asking your advice? Do you fear the Lord, serving him faithfully and remembering the great things He has done for you? Write down the things (big and small) that God does for you, and share those things with your children. Are you keeping your relationship with the Lord intimate through Bible reading and honest conversation with Him? Are you praying for and with your children? First Samuel 12:24 is a great prayer for your kids. Teach them to pray by your example. Pray about the little things in their lives and watch God increase their faith.

Lastly, are you trusting God? He is trustworthy, you know. He really does love your children more than you do—hard to believe, but true. Give your children to the Lord in your heart—acknowledge that they are His precious gifts entrusted to you for a short while. Then, through the years, release them back to Him. What an awesome opportunity you have to glorify God by loving His treasures and releasing them to serve Him, wherever and however that may be.

✥ Michele Calvert ✥

Michele Calvert's day revolves around kids. She is presently the children's church coordinator at Memorial Bible Church in Yakima, Washington, and has served as MOPS coordinator for six years. Michele believes that "God has given me the greatest discipleship opportunity in life with my three wonderful children, Charis, Cady, and Connor."

A Mother's Translation of Scripture

One day several men were discussing which translation of the Bible they preferred. After the popular debate, one said, "Frankly, I've always liked my mother's translation the best." With some surprise, the others said, "We didn't know your mother had translated the Bible."

"Yes, she did," he said. "She translated it into her life every day she lived. And it was through her translation I came to faith in the Son of the God."

When eternity comes and the secrets are unveiled, I have no doubt but that the greatest soul winners in the world will be the mothers who led their children lovingly and authentically to a saving knowledge of Jesus Christ. As any mother knows, words go in one ear and out the other. But ladies, we just cannot forget your life.

Chuck Swindoll

A Working Woman's Guide to Survival

By Colette Smith

Juggling your relationships and home life with a career? Get a godly perspective of how to be a woman of balance and godly priorities.

Twenty minutes into an important meeting, I received a note from the receptionist stating that I needed to call home *IMMEDIATELY.* Embarrassed to be an interruption but in a mild state of panic, I excused myself and ran back to my office to call my husband.

"I need to go to the doctor," is all he said.

It was all he needed to say. In four years of marriage, Mark had never seen a doctor. Understanding that it had to be serious, I assured him, "I'll be right there."

When I got home, I found Mark lying on floor trying to catch his breath. He was stark white and his 6'2" frame was shaking. I called my doctor, and she agreed to meet us at the hospital.

After several tests and an EKG, my doctor asked Mark if he was experiencing a lot of stress. His reply was, "not really." At that moment, I snapped. I started laughing. The doctor and my husband looked at one another confused. I was unable to control myself, and in a minute the laughter turned to streaming tears.

How was it that my husband was unable to admit that the stress in our life had become almost insurmountable? It had been months since we laughed together, and lately we barely touched. I considered infertility, a struggling home business, a mountain of unfinished house projects, and a job that had me frequently traveling — "a lot of stress."

And what's worse, we felt like God was nowhere to be found. We prayed for answers and were slowly realizing He wasn't going to send us a quick fix. On top of our obvious circumstances, our inner turmoil was killing us.

The doctor told Mark that he had experienced a panic attack. Frankly, I was surprised I hadn't had one long ago. The trip home was silent. My husband was humiliated, and we felt exhausted, defeated, and angry. We knew that the suffocating blanket of stress needed to be lifted. We desired to be content but didn't know how.

I know we are not alone. Unlike many men who can function quite well until they reach a breaking point, women usually carry the bulk of their worries with them every minute of everyday. We pack them in our purses and briefcases with our daily planners or palm pilots. We keep thinking that we'll find contentment somewhere between the completed deadlines and successful meetings. But each day, *be content* shows up on our to-do list.

For those of us who work, that search for contentment and relief seems especially daunting. We struggle with our priorities and often feel like we don't live up to our own expectations, let alone God's. We look to our models in Scripture that support our view that women (as well as men) receive callings from God, but we are lost in deciphering the priority that calling takes in our lives.

A brief look at the women of the Bible and it's clear to see how God calls—and effectively uses women in the work-place. Remember the familiar Proverbs 31 model woman? (If you're like me, you have a love/hate relationship with her. When does she sleep?) She maintains a healthy self-image, a suc-cessful marriage, balanced family life, even a min-istry to others—all the while being extremely effective on the job. Take a look at the Proverbs 31 model on the following page.

> Whether He tells you directly or through circumstance that working outside the home is where He wants you, then listen and embrace the place of influence where He has put you.

Because of the example of the Proverbs 31 woman and others represented in the Bible (see Acts 16:13–15; 17:4,12 for more work-ing women), I feel called to do what I do. I enjoy what I do, and I am good at what I do. But, it hasn't always been that clear. Through the closing of one door after another, God has led me to realize that He has me where He wants me, and that is at the office.

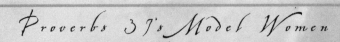

Proverbs 31's Model Women

Her godly attitude and perspective overflow into her relationships:

- Strength and dignity are her clothing, and she smiles at the future. (v. 25)

- She opens her mouth in wisdom, and the teaching of kindness is on her tongue. (v. 26)

She cares about her physical appearance, yet keeps her personal priorities in check:

- She makes coverings for herself; her clothing is fine linen and purple. (v. 22)

- Charm is deceitful and beauty is vain, but a woman who fears the Lord, she shall be praised. (v. 30)

Her relationship with her husband and family benefits, not suffers, from her involvements.

- The heart of her husband trusts in her, and he will have no lack of gain. (v. 11)

- She does him good and not evil all the days of her life. (v. 12)

- She is not afraid of the snow for her household, for all her household are clothed with scarlet. (v. 21)

- She looks well to the ways of her household, and does not eat the bread of idleness. (v. 27)

- Her children rise up and bless her; her husband also, and he praises her. (v. 28)

She is an industrious, savvy, wise career woman:

- She looks for wool and flax and works with her hands in delight. (v. 13)

- She is like merchant ships; she brings her food from afar. (v. 14)

- She rises also while it is still night and gives food to her household and portions to her maidens. (v. 15)

- She considers a field and buys it; from her earnings she plants a vineyard. (v. 16)

- She girds herself with strength and makes her arms strong. (v. 17)

- She senses that her gain is good; her lamp does not go out at night. (v. 18)

- She stretches out her hands to the distaff, and her hands grasp the spindle. (v. 19)

- She makes linen garments and sells them, and supplies belts to the tradesmen. (v. 24)

She even has a heart for ministry.

- She extends her hand to the poor, and she stretches out her hands to the needy. (v. 20)

Has God also called you to the office? Too often we're told another story. *A woman's place is in the home—exclusively.* A brief look at Proverbs 31 tells us differently. It also tells us a lot about priorities.

On the way home from the hospital with Mark, it would have been easy to blame my job for the stress that we were facing. I could have dreamed of quitting and making our lives rosy with the fantasy of becoming a domestic goddess. Secretly I've always wondered if fresh sheets and a spotless floor were the answers to all of life's dilemmas. But the truth is, my work was the only area that we could hear God's voice speaking loud and clear.

My order of priorities have become clearer these days.

For one, I realize the importance of perspective. I would love to tell you that over the course of a year, the circumstances that caused our stress have vanished. But they haven't. What's changed is how we're looking at them. In numerous ways, we see God providing for us. Practically speaking, He has given us my job to keep us afloat. We see this time as an adventure in faith, and that perspective welcomes frequent laughter and surprise in our home.

This gift of perspective has taught us to see "big things—big and small things—small." Perhaps this list, though limited, will help you discern your big and little things:

Embrace your calling. Accountant, administrative assistant, missionary, doctor, full-time homemaker—God calls us each to different opportunities. There is no formula for serving Him. Whether He tells you directly or through circumstance that working outside the home is where He wants you, then listen and embrace the place of influence where He has put you.

Pray about it. It all starts here. Bring your day, your life, your job to Him. He is your source of strength. If your call begins with Him, then let Him lead it every step of the way. Pray about your decisions, your interactions, your time, and your motives. Pray about your failures and your triumphs. Start when you are getting out of bed and don't end until your head hits the pillow. Give it all to Him; He's ready.

Remember your mission. Luke 10:38–42 is a perfect example of losing God's call in the midst of details. Martha was confused; it wasn't that the details were wrong, it was her focus. Don't allow yourself to get trapped in the details of your life and lose His purpose. Make time to sit at His feet and worship.

Take good care of yourself. Shortly after Mark's panic attack, we realized that our stress had kept us from the very thing that could help us manage it—exercise. We recommitted to eating healthy, and we're back into our regular physical routine. I am certain this essential helps us keep balance in our busy lives.

Let it go. I've spent a better part of my working life worrying about the dishes in the sink and the unmade bed at home. I struggle with the feeling that if I can't completely have my personal life in order, I don't have much to offer to the outside world. While this seems a bit silly (and admittedly downright obsessive), what similar unreasonable expectations are you setting for yourself?

My good friend Darcy found herself in a similar situation. She makes a decent salary and feels genuinely called to work. Yet, she felt guilty about hiring someone to help her with the domestic duties in running a household. Darcy's first experience with a maid was a gift from her mother. Darcy realized that what seemed extravagant to her, helps her give in other areas. While we all can't afford housecleaning, what are the areas that you need to ask for help? What can you give up in order to give more to your self, your family, or your ministry?

Make strategic decisions. In our professional lives, we make hard decisions everyday. We prioritize workloads and negotiate deadlines. Yet, many women feel powerless to do the same in their personal lives. Learn to think before committing, make wise decisions, and say "no" to certain activities, so you'll be ready to say "yes" to the important ones.

Take a break. If God took a day off to rest after creating the world, then we would do well to follow His example. In order to be a balanced worker, we need time to view our work in perspective. We need time to enjoy our families, our friends, and ourselves. We need time alone to think, to pray, to play. A day (or occasionally a week) off will only boost our creativity and make us better workers.

I pray you, too, will find contentment in where God calls you. Like me, your circumstances may not be all that you imagined, but there is peace when you recognize He is at work. Seek Him, give Him your dreams, your fears, and especially your talents. Offer what you are and what you do as a sacrifice to God and ask Him to use it for His glory—whatever that will be.

Above all, may we be women who can be called "virtuous, excellent, blessed, and one who fears the Lord."

> *May the loveliness of the Lord our God rest upon us; confirming the work that we do. Oh, yes. Affirm the work that we do!* (Psalm 90:17, The Message)

⋙ Colette Smith ⋘

*W*ith a passion for living purposefully and creatively, Colette Smith extends her enthusiasm to her role of marketing manager at Insight for Living. Colette wishes "that working women would embrace their God-given calling to shine for Him in whatever circumstance He places them in." She and her husband Mark live in Yorba Linda, California where they are raising their yellow Lab, Cabo.

Ladies, are you convinced of your value in God's eyes? God's Book does a great job to eclipse the lies, the lack of vision, and the lack of praise to which our culture often defaults. Need a good chapter to read—try Proverbs 31.

Why not try this—read Proverbs 31 every day with an eye towards the confidence God places in you. Be challenged by the character traits found within these 31 verses: industriousness, vision, a balanced independence, wisdom, confidence, class, dignity, accomplishment, and a positive attitude. Can you find each one in these verses? I challenge you to pick one and claim it for God. By His grace, ask Him to make it true in your life this year.

Chuck Swindoll

> Strength and dignity are her clothing, and she smiles at the future (v. 25).
> Charm is deceitful and beauty is vain, but a woman who fears the Lord, she shall be praised (v. 30).

DISCOVERING THE MINISTRY OF LEADERSHIP

By JoAnn Hummel

"How do you hope God will use you as a leader in ministry?"

The question came from a seasoned servant of God and for the first time prompted me to consider the concept of my own leadership. That day, I stammered something about how I hoped God would use me to shepherd women in a local church setting. That incident was almost fifteen years ago. Since then I have served as a leader to women and have gained insight—at times surprisingly—into the leadership task.

Perhaps you have had or will have the opportunity to be used by God as a spiritual leader to women. Your leadership could take many forms, but some common principles apply if you desire your leadership to impact lives for years to come.

Principle #1—Learn all you can about yourself

In 1 Timothy 3:1, Paul commends the individual who desires to lead others by calling that desire *noble*. The following six verses (vv. 2–7) list the qualities a leader ought to exhibit.

To highlight a few: As a woman who desires to lead, you need to be above reproach, temperate, self-controlled, respectable, hospitable, able to teach, gentle, not quarrelsome, not a lover of money, a good manager of your family, a mature believer, and a person of good reputation.

Paul's list of leadership qualities requires that you know yourself—both your areas of giftedness and weakness. Over the years, I have been prompted to discover what makes me tick. Surprisingly, this process of self-examination has proven to be a leadership-altering experience. Perhaps you can see yourself in some of my personal examples.

Am I the right person for this job?

The church where I serve defines ministry in the fast lane. For a long time, I was plagued by suspicions that I was the wrong person for the job. Learning, however, that my preferred pace is much slower has freed me to build times for solitude into my life, and these times balance the hectic but exciting ride that church ministry can be.

What is my vision for ministry?

Our senior pastor is gripped with a wide vision. Without breaking a sweat, Pete can talk about our church having 100,000 members someday. However, I hear his "visioning" and often feel faint.

Over the years, I have learned that I also have vision, but my vision is deep rather than wide. My passion runs hot for individuals to be connected and known. Rather than competing, these visions complement each other and are vital to the health of the church.

What kind of ministry colleagues will complement my leadership?

I am an inventor. New ways of conceptualizing ministry programs excite me. Arm me with a marker and a clean surface and I will sketch out my dreams with boundless enthusiasm. But implementing those dreams is another matter completely. Knowing this bent in my leadership has guided me in recruiting ministry colleagues. I purposefully pray for and search out women whose assets complement my deficits. As an inventor, I need implementers—women who can put feet to the vision and make it run!

In a meeting several weeks ago, the importance of having complementary colleagues struck me afresh. While I passionately explained some ideas to emphasize discipleship and spiritual formation in our existing women's small groups, I could tell from my two colleagues' expressions that they were thinking, *Yeah, but how?* When I was called away for a few minutes I returned to see them huddled knee-to-knee, evaluating, discussing, and planning the how-to of the vision. If I labored under the false idea that a leader has to be the perfect package, I would have missed God's powerfully shaping the inventor's vision through the implementer's eye for detail.

> *If I labored under the false idea that a leader has to be the perfect package, I would have missed God's powerfully shaping the inventor's vision through the implementer's eye for detail.*

Self-knowledge is a lifelong process that nourishes our hunger to seek God. John Calvin wrote, "Without knowledge of self there is no knowledge of God. Through the knowledge of ourselves and our condition, we are aroused to seek God." Far from being selfish, knowing yourself will enhance your leadership experience.

Principle #2—Empower others to serve

Ephesians 4:11–12 describes leaders as those who prepare God's people for works of service. But I was hired in ministry because I am a doer. On becoming a ministry leader, however, I discovered that the doer had to somehow morph into an equipper—and my transition from doer to equipper has not been all that smooth.

Our church is in a metroplex area, and our body of believers is busy and upwardly mobile. Consequently, I was afraid to ask people to serve in ministry. Fearing to "shoulder tap" anyone, I locked myself into "doer mode". On Sunday mornings, I would arrive early to sort children's toys in the classrooms and resupply the adult rooms with tissues, erasers, and markers. I would straighten chairs, haul podiums, and bundle up the nursery laundry to wash at home. Far from being the servant leader I thought I was, I was actually preventing others from operating in their giftedness by doing every job.

This principle of empowering others to serve hit home as I was decorating a hallway bulletin board. Pulling a colorful border from its plastic sleeve, I looked up to see Frank, one of our elders, striding towards me. He looked serious. Placing his hands on my shoulders, Frank looked me squarely in the eyes and said, "JoAnn, we need you to lead around here." Then he released his grip, turned, and walked away.

My brief encounter with Frank is changing the way I lead. Slowly but surely, I am growing into a leader who shepherds, trains, and empowers others to serve Christ. The way I see it now is that if I don't ask people to serve, I am robbing them of rich spiritual blessings. What's more, I have been amazed to discover that when the ministry task requires many individuals, people will rise to the occasion with grace and increasing faith.

It's common to hear ministry professionals complain that you just can't get volunteers anymore. I wonder sometimes if those who lead are addicted doers. Doers whine that they need help but never ask or empower others to take on the tasks.

Timothy was shoulder-tapped by Paul to shepherd the church at Ephesus. In 1 Timothy 4:11–16, Timothy was empowered by Paul's affirmations and commands. "Teach these things." "Devote yourself." "Set an example." "Persevere." Paul assigned Ephesus to Timothy and stoked Timothy's inner fire to get the job done. By the Spirit's power, Timothy flourished as a pastoral leader. How many Timothys are waiting for you to invite them into service and make their own mark?

Honestly, I miss the old "hands-on" days. It's a risk to let go and invite others to make their mark. But it's a risk worth taking. The next time you're asked to tackle a certain job, why not consider someone you could tap on the shoulder? Then, equip and empower her to eventually take the lead.

Principle #3 — Abide in Christ

Leaders do not always luxuriate in an experience of spiritual freshness. Sometimes life is a walking tour through Ezekiel's valley of dry bones. The past several months have been that dry for me. When you couple the physical pain of surgery with the emotional stress of family problems, you have a one way ticket to the spiritual desert.

The leadership lesson I am learning from these desert days is that God's grip on me is fierce. The word *abide* pictures God's loving grasp on me in spite of my frail hold on Him.

John 15 is the text that unfolds this awesome and mystical relationship of dependence—Jesus, the vine, and His believers, the branches. The story is one of fruitfulness but hidden there among the leaves and branches is another lesson as well. The branch does not cling to the vine; no, the vine's very life provides the source for the branch to stay connected. As the branch remains in the life source of the vine, it will be fruitful.

Fruit-bearing has its seasons. Spring and summer mean foliage and fruit, and fall is the harvest. But abiding is not seasonal. To survive throughout the seasons, the branch must abide, or remain connected—however feebly—to the vine.

Remember the last time you drew near to God in humility and need? What did you find? More than likely, you discovered that God was drawing near to you too. In fact, He initiated your intimate overtures. Abiding in Christ is so crucial—especially when we realize how many people are drawing strength from us!

My dog, Buttons, is an apt picture of the abiding life. Recently, she became very sick and I took her to the emergency clinic. Although she could barely hold up her head and walk straight, she did her best to stay right by my side each step. When I realized she lacked the strength to keep up, I bent down and lifted her up. I carried her from the car into the clinic. When Buttons could barely hold on, I held on to her.

Could I be so presumptuous and ask you to imitate my dog? Abide in Christ, leader. And someday, when you can barely hang on to Him, you will experience the abiding love and power of Jesus holding on to you.

Leadership That Grows

Do you notice a common thread tying these principles together? Each principle presupposes continuous effort *but not completion.*

- Learning about yourself is a lifelong project.
- Empowering others to serve demands constant prayer and encouragement.
- Abiding in Christ by its very nature describes a continuous relationship.

I stay on track when I focus on *becoming* a leader instead of *being* the leader. Becoming a leader reminds me that I have not arrived.

"How do you hope God will use you as a leader in ministry?" Your answers to this question could be as deep and wide as the myriad of ministry avenues. However, these three practical principles hold true in all facets of godly leadership. May they be used to encourage you as we each grow in wisdom and skill, dependent on God for His ministry through us to the women He has called us to serve.

⇒ JoAnn Hummel ⇐

A gifted communicator and teacher, JoAnn Hummel speaks and writes with humor, sensitivity, and insight to the unique needs of Christian women. A graduate of Dallas Theological Seminary and in her ninth year in leadership over Women's Ministries and Pastoral Care at Bent Tree Bible Fellowship in Carrollton, Texas, JoAnn says, "My greatest joy as a leader is to watch other women lead and succeed!"

Public Ministries of Women in the Bible

❧ Deborah led God's people in wisdom and courage during the days of the judges. **Judges 4:9**

❧ Abigail interceded on her husband's behalf and made peace with David. She served David and his men a feast in gratitude for their protection. **1 Samuel 25:18–35**

❧ When Jesus ministered in different cities around the land, the disciples followed Him, as did a handful of women—Mary Magdalene, Joanna, Susanna, and others—who contributed to the disciples' support out of their own means. **Luke 8:1–3**

❧ The testimony of the woman at the well drew many Samaritan men and women to Jesus **John 4:39–42**

❧ Mary and Martha of Bethany frequently opened their household to Jesus when He and His disciples visited Jerusalem. **John 11**

❧ Tabitha, who was always doing good and helping the poor, often by sewing them clothes, was raised from the dead by Peter. **Acts 9:36–46**

❧ The apostles ministered to and were served by a number of prominent women on their missionary journeys. **Acts 16:13–15; 17:4, 12**

Continued on next page

Public Ministries of Women in the Bible

Continued from previous page

❧ Lydia, a businesswoman from Thyatira, welcomed the apostles and followers of Jesus to meet in her home as a regular place of worship and instruction. **Acts 16:14**

❧ Priscilla, well-versed in doctrine, hosted the first Bible studies in her home with her husband, Aquila. They helped instruct and build the early church. **Romans 16:3-5**

❧ Paul urged two ladies, Euodia and Syntyche, "who shared [his] struggle in the cause of the gospel," to please get along with each other in the Lord. **Philippians 4:2-3**

❧ John's second letter was dedicated to "the chosen lady" and her children, who served the body of Christ. **2 John**

Women Helping Women: Lifestyle Mentorship

by Vickie Kraft

Being married, experienced, successful, or beautiful is not the criteria used to assess your potential for ministry—having a heart for God and people is what matters.

God turned my life around when I was twenty-eight and married with a two-and-a-half-year-old son. My husband and I were attending a Christian conference for a week, asking God to heal our hearts and the turmoil in our marriage. Early one morning, I stood on the porch of our little cabin and cried out to God that if He couldn't make a consistent, stable Christian out of me, I just didn't want to live any longer. The pain was too great.

When I returned home from the conference, God answered my prayer through two women whose examples helped guide me into future ministry. My sister, involved with the Navigators in California that previous year, shared with me, "I've learned an exciting new way to study the Bible. Would you like me to teach you how to do it?" Of course, I was interested, and she showed me how to study and look for a specific personal application from the text for the purpose of obeying it. That was my beginning—to find encouragement, instruction, and guidance from the Word of God. This led to memorizing Scripture, which prepares our minds so the Holy Spirit can use His

Word for our benefit as well as others'.

I began attending a Bible study taught by a single lady about eighteen years my senior. She taught with wisdom, compassion, and a thorough knowledge of God's Word. One day, she asked if I would be willing to teach a Bible study for a woman whom she had led to Christ from a cult. I taught that class in her home and presence for five years, and though she could have done a far better job than me, she participated as a member of the class. She prayed for me, taught me biblical truths, and encouraged me. That class set me on the path toward full-time ministry God had prepared for me—a full-time ministry that emphasizes motivating and equipping women to live for God's glory.

God answered my desperate prayer by sending two special women, one a peer and one older, to equip me for His purpose for my life. Though I didn't realize it then, they had followed the biblical pattern for spiritual discipleship or mentoring—they were faithful teachers and role models of the instructions Paul left for a young pastor:

> *Older women likewise are to be reverent in their behavior, not malicious gossips nor enslaved to much wine, teaching what is good, so that they may encourage the young women to love their husbands, to love their children, to be sensible, pure, workers at home, kind, being subject to their own husbands, so that the word of God will not be dishonored.* (Titus 2:3–5)

A Mentor's Credentials

Women today need to know that they are valuable; they were created in God's image and bought with a great price—the life of His Son.

Being married, successful, or beautiful, therefore, is not the criteria used to assess one's potential for ministry. We may not all have a public speaking ministry, but we can all minister individually to the young women in our lives. Young women long for these relationships, but many older women— usually equipped to do this well—often are the least confident. They assume they must be Bible scholars to be able to mentor, but all that's needed is a working knowledge of Scripture, the source of our worldview.

We may not all have a public-speaking ministry, but we can all minister individually to the young women in our lives.

Paul's curriculum is very practical; it affects every area of a woman's life—her character, her family, her homemaking skills, her community impact. The "older woman" he spoke of may be a wonderful cook, a creative homemaker, or a successful career woman. She may have an enduring marriage, a family, and children who walk with the Lord. Or she may have children who aren't. She may be divorced or she may have never married. She may have endured serious illnesses or given care to her elderly parents. What matters is that she leaned on the Lord for comfort, strength, and grace through it all. Her life experiences equipped her with empathy and wisdom. They are her credentials as a mentor, a role model, and a teacher—a spiritual mother to younger women who want to mature in their faith.

Why has God assigned this vital ministry to women? Several reasons. First, we can do it because we know how it feels to go through experiences uniquely a woman's. Only a woman can both model and teach what it looks like for a woman to live for God's glory. Second, we can follow up and nurture a friendship with calls, visits, and accountability. When women counsel women, the opportunity for temptation men might face is avoided.

So, the mentoring woman should be older, but she should also be above reproach. She's trustworthy and not addicted to external substances or activities to help her cope with pain. And she is "reverent," Paul said, implying that she views life as sacred and doesn't divide sacred from secular in her everyday life. She approaches each of her responsibilities as opportunities for ministry that bring glory to God, whether it be keeping her home, raising children, showing hospitality, helping those in need, or having a career.

A Mentor's Curriculum

Now, what is the older woman to teach those following her?

She emphasizes *personal character*. Women are to be "sensible," "pure," and "kind," meaning they live wisely; they commit to celibacy before marriage, fidelity in marriage, and a healthy thought life; and they show concern for others. The mentor, therefore, models discretion, encourages pure living, and exemplifies love for the younger woman to follow.

She also emphasizes the *integrity* and *health* of the family. Wives are to "love their husbands"—love them with human emotion, friendship, pleasure, and enjoyment. After God, her husband comes first in her heart and life. She is "subject" to his leadership as an expression of her obedience to Jesus Christ. This loyal support makes his job easier and provides an atmosphere of peace in the home. She submits to his leadership as he encourages her to reach her full potential.

In a day when children run the risks of being killed in the womb, neglected, molested, abused, or abandoned after birth, God's command that women "love their children" is especially appropriate. Young children should be the priority over a career at this stage in life. The single mother who must work to support her family may find alternative ways to provide income so that she can give her children the attention they need. God values the emotional and spiritual development of children more than possessions or status. The ministry of homemaking elevates our dreariest tasks to spiritual service.

A Mentor's Comfort

How farsighted is the biblical curriculum of Titus 2! The results of violating these principles can be seen in our society today, and it is even more essential for Christian women to swim against the current and follow these clear commands. The result will be nothing short of emotional, psychological, and spiritual health for our families and ourselves.

If our families and personal lives reflect this pattern, we will also have a positive impact on our community. Our lives will honor the Lord and demonstrate the truths of Scripture. Others will be hungry for what we enjoy, and they will be more receptive to the gospel.

God created women to be influential. We influence our husbands, children, friends, church, and society. We must determine that our influence will be godly, and it is a privilege to join God in His work among women. Choosing to be role models and mentors for the women in our lives will encourage and equip them to live for God's glory. God's grace in my own life testifies to that fact.

✦ Vickie Kraft ✦

Vickie Kraft is president of Titus 2:4 Ministries, which exists to teach, motivate, and encourage women to mentor the generations following them so that they will live to please God. For thirteen years, Vickie led women's ministry at Northwest Bible Church in Dallas, Texas. Vickie says, "I saw the dynamic of women mentoring younger women fleshed out year after year, bringing blessings to the whole church."

Devote yourselves to prayer, keeping alert in it with an attitude of thanksgiving. . . .

Conduct yourselves with wisdom toward outsiders, making the most of the opportunity. *Let your speech always be with grace,* as though seasoned with salt, so that you will know how you should respond to each person.

Colossians 4:2, 5–6

A
Heart
That's His

THE REASON FOR MY JOY

by Luci Swindoll

Need a reason to smile? Pay careful attention to the joys of your everyday life and be transformed by your loving, gracious, wonderful, perfectly outrageous God.

In my closet, I have a plaid skirt that's over twenty-five years old, five sizes too small, and quite out of style. Believe me, there's no chance I'll ever wear it again. Not on your life. But will I discard it? Not on your life. My daddy gave it to me.

Anything from him, I plan to keep. Although he's been dead eighteen years, he's still very much alive in my mind. He was a wonderful man: competent, tender, funny, intelligent, and full of wisdom. I thought he was the greatest guy on the planet.

The two of us enjoyed a "mutual admiration society." One year I was trying to decide what to give him for his birthday, and my brothers suggested a framed picture of myself, candles, and matches. "Since he worships you anyway," they reasoned, "he could build a little shrine."

Daddy gave me tangible gifts, and many intangible ones as well. I received letters from him every week when I was away at college, and for years afterward while I worked in another city. The letters were laced with love, encouragement from God's Word, and profound understanding of me—not only as his daughter, but also as a person.

He had my best interest at heart and made that very clear, all the time. By his lavish giving, unconditional love, and awareness of my deepest needs, Daddy was all the cheering squad I ever needed. Because of him, I had an excellent model of a gracious, caring heavenly Father.

Although we don't all have that kind of earthly model of love and affection, everybody who is a child of God has a heavenly Father who exceeds all expectations and imagination. My dad may have seemed like the ringleader of our home, but the reason he was such a great parent was he knew the true Ringleader intimately. It was my father's relationship with Christ that made him such a quality person.

Each of us who knows Christ personally can relate to a perfect heavenly Father and become more like Him every day. That's incredible! When we become part of God's family, we immediately receive numerous gifts. To name just a few . . .

- We're set free from an unrelenting law to experience unmerited grace (Romans 6:14; Galatians 3:25).

- We're given immediate access to the throne of God for praise or petition (Hebrews 4:14–16).

- We're indwelled by the Spirit of God and guaranteed His presence in all our heartaches and temptations (1 Corinthians 6:19; 2 Corinthians 1:21–22).

- We're promised a life that never ends and a glorious home in heaven (1 John 5:11).

- We're given a job to do that has an eternal purpose (Matthew 28:19).

- We're forgiven of everything we ever did wrong (Ephesians 1:7; Colossians 1:13–14).

- We're assured that all our needs will be met (Philippians 4:19).

- We're promised that God will never leave us or forsake us (Psalm 37:25; Hebrews 13:5).

These are only the tip of the iceberg of gifts that become ours. And get this—they're free! All these gifts are given to us simply because we believe what God said, receive what God did, and are now recipients of who God is—the giver of abundant, eternal life.

There is nothing average about the God we know, the Father we long to serve. He's unconventional and exorbitant. He's extravagant in His giving. He's unrestrained in His love for us. In fact, God is extraordinary in every way. He's outrageous! If you and I were to catch even a glimpse of who He is, our lives would never be the same. And yet, He's shown us who He is. His truth and glory are revealed in His Son, Jesus Christ. And we see it every day in the universe He created, in the lives of others, and in our own experiences. We often miss it, but it's there. We just forget to notice.

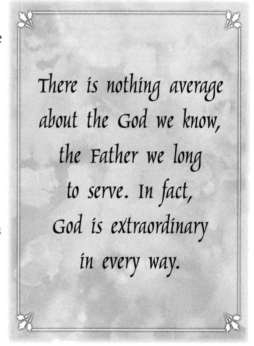

There is nothing average about the God we know, the Father we long to serve. In fact, God is extraordinary in every way.

Let's notice. Let's pay careful attention. Let's let our everyday lives be invaded and transformed by this loving, gracious, wonderful, perfectly outrageous God.

The joy He provides is outrageous because it is completely unencumbered by the circumstances we face.

His grace is outrageous as well. It is unmerited, unwarranted, undeserved, and unrelenting. His Word says, "Yet to all who received Him, to those who believed in His name, He gave the right to become children of God" (John 1:12).

And peace! The Bible promises, "And the peace of God, which transcends all understanding, will guard your hearts and your minds in Christ Jesus" (Philippians 4:7). Whose life wouldn't be transformed if she experienced that kind of peace no matter what was happening?

And just think about His love. It never ends. It never even wavers. The apostle Paul thrilled at this outrageous thought: "For I am convinced that neither death nor life, neither angels nor demons, neither the present nor the future, nor any powers, neither height nor depth, nor anything else in all creation, will be able to separate us from the love of God that is in Christ Jesus our Lord" (Romans 8:38–39).

And freedom? Now this is fabulous! We have freedom from the law, freedom in Christ, freedom to be all we were created to be. "It is for freedom that Christ has set us free. Stand firm, then, and do not let yourselves be burdened again by a yoke of slavery" (Galatians 5:1).

There's *no* question about God giving us outrageous hope. Hope enables us to feel the intangible, imagine the invisible, and achieve the impossible. We believe God keeps His promises, and with confidence we wait for them to be fulfilled. What God told His people through the prophet Jeremiah is still true for us today: " 'For I know the plans I have for you,' declares the Lord, 'plans to prosper you and not to harm you, plans to give you hope and a future'" (Jeremiah 29:11).

God's whole plan to reconcile the human race to Himself was outrageous. It was inevitable that His own Son would be outrageous too! Jesus was a man of paradoxes who shocked, surprised, incensed, or delighted everyone He met. As His followers, we shouldn't be surprised that our lives will take some outrageous twists and turns, or that we will sometimes stand out as "circus freaks" in a world that doesn't recognize our glorious nature in Christ. As Thelma [Wells] puts it, to be a woman of faith means that "your elevator doesn't go to the top floor. Your clock ticks in a counterclockwise direction. Your cart is before the horse. And your joy is always ignited in spite of your delicate condition."

If we really took God at His Word and lived out the implications of these outrageous attributes, our lives would be characterized by what Eugene Peterson calls "the plain meaning of the message of Christ." There would much more than mere moral reformation in us; our lives would be utterly transformed! We'd be like the early Christians whose humdrum human lives became linked to the very life of God Himself—the divine Ringleader of the whole shebang. It was then, if you recall, they turned the world upside down.

Grasp the outrageous truth: God is here. God is now. And He longs to pour out all of who He is into your life every day. His life can be in you and flow through you. Outrageous!

✦ Luci Swindoll ✦

"*L*oving God. Loving others. Loving yourself. They're all bound together with the cords of our heavenly Father's great design and objective," says speaker and author Luci Swindoll. Earlier in her career, Luci served as an executive at Mobil Oil Corporation, then as vice president of public relations at IFL. Today, she lives in California and continues to touch lives though her vigorous speaking schedule with Women of Faith.

Sixteen Different Ways Proverbs
Describes a Woman . . .

"Understanding will watch over you . . .
To guard you from *the strange woman*" (2:11a, 16a).

"Let your fountain be blessed
And rejoice in the *wife* of your youth" (5:18).

"Reproofs for discipline are the way of life
To keep you from the *evil woman*" (6:23b–24a).

"For on account of a *harlot* one is reduced to a loaf
of bread,
And an *adulteress* hunts for the precious life" (6:26).

"A gracious *woman* attains honor" (11:16a).

"As a ring of gold in a swine's snout
So is a *beautiful woman who lacks discretion*" (11:22).

"The *wise woman* builds her house,
But the *foolish* tears it down with her own hands"
(14:1).

Continued on next page

Sixteen Different Ways Proverbs
Describes a Woman ...

Continued from previous page

"The Lord will tear down the house of the proud
But He will establish the boundary of the *widow*"
(15:25).

"House and wealth are an inheritance from fathers,
But a *prudent wife* is from the Lord" (19:14).

"Listen to your father who begot you,
And do not despise your *mother* when she is old"
(23:22).

"A constant dripping on a day of steady rain
And a *contentious woman* are alike" (27:15).

"This is the way of an *adulterous woman*:
She eats and wipes her mouth,
And says, 'I have done no wrong'" (30:20).

"Many *daughters* have done nobly,
But you excel them all" (31:29).

"An *excellent wife*, who can find?
For her worth is far above jewels" (31:10).

FACING THE ENEMY IN PRAYER

by Ney Bailey

Three life-changing characteristics about prayer will transform your life. Learn to pray like Jesus prayed and discover how different life can be.

I remember when I first began to learn about spiritual warfare. One day I said, "Lord, teach me to pray." I remembered these were the words the disciples used that prompted Jesus to teach them what we refer to as the Lord's Prayer. As I was praying through that prayer, I noticed the line that reads, "Lead us not into temptation, but deliver us from the evil one" (Matthew 6:13 NIV). It had never occurred to me to pray for deliverance from the Evil One before, and I wondered if I should be doing it all the time, since Jesus indicated it was to be a daily prayer.

Jesus prayed a similar prayer in John 17 when He told the Father, "I do not ask You to take [the disciples] out of the world, but to keep them from the evil one" (v. 15). And so I realized that when I pray to be delivered from the Evil One, I am agreeing with Jesus that the Father will keep me from him. I've been praying the Lord's Prayer every day since then, for the past twenty-five years.

We're in a position of authority over the Evil One because

Ephesians 1–2 teaches that we've been raised with Christ and are seated with Him in the heavenlies. It tells us we're "seated . . . far above all rule and authority and power and dominion, and every name that is named" (1:20–21). And it's from that position that we battle in spiritual warfare.

Ephesians 6 addresses that warfare directly: "Finally, be strong in the Lord and in the strength of His might. Put on the full armor of God, so that you will be able to stand firm against the schemes of the devil" (vv. 10–11). Though we faithfully don the armor of God each day for this battle, the end of Paul's letter names prayer as our continual weapon for warfare: "With all prayer and petition pray at all times in the Spirit" (v. 18).

So, we pray at all times. But for what do we pray? How are we going to be "strong in the Lord and in the strength of His might" through prayer? Christ taught the disciples that lesson not long after He taught them the Lord's Prayer. He taught them to be consistent in prayer, and He taught them to knock and seek and ask in prayer, but He ended those lessons with this word of admonition:

> *"Now suppose one of you fathers is asked by his son for a fish; he will not give him a snake instead of a fish, will he? Or if he is asked for an egg, he will not give him a scorpion, will he? If you then, being evil, know how to give good gifts to your children, how much more will your heavenly Father give the Holy Spirit to those who ask Him?"* (Luke 11:11–13)

This verse changed Oswald Chambers' life. It's etched into his tombstone because he banked his life on it and asked to be filled with the Holy Spirit every day. When I found that out, I told myself,

"Well, if it's good enough for Oswald Chambers, it's good enough for me." In Ephesians 5:18, we are commanded to be filled with the Holy Spirit. So every morning I began to pray, "Father, I ask You in Jesus' name to fill me with Your Spirit."

Not long after I discovered this treasure in prayer, John Stott preached at our little church in Oxford, England, where I was staying for two years. He said that every day for twenty-five years he had been praying not only to be filled with the Spirit but to be filled with the fruit of the Spirit. So I added that to my daily prayer: "Father, I pray You would fill me with Your love and Your joy and Your peace and Your patience, Your kindness, Your goodness, Your faith-fulness, Your gentleness, and Your self-control."

> *If the Lord gives you the ability to see something that's not honoring to the Lord, use that discernment for the purpose of prayer.*

The Lord has taught me several life-changing things about prayer since I began praying those prayers every day. The first is to **pray specifically**. Matthew 20:29–34 recounts Jesus' encounter with two blind men on the road. He was walking close enough to touch them and could see that they were blind, but He asked them, "What do you want Me to do for you?" And it wasn't until they said, "Lord, we want our eyes to be opened" that He was moved to touch their eyes and give them sight. If the Lord Himself would make a blind man be specific in his request, how much more does He desire us to be specific with ours! We need to pray beyond the vague "Well, Lord, you know" kind of prayers we often say. We need to be specific.

Second, we need to **turn discernment into intercessory prayer**. My friend Jean Pietsch and I traveled eight states together in the south-central region of the United States. One time we traveled to minister on a campus with another team of Christians. When we got there, the oppression of unhealthy relationships among the team members was strong. There was tension. There were troubles. And we felt very burdened about it. That first night, we slipped out to talk about the needs we discerned and then decided to lift them up in prayer. We prayed specifically over each situation, each relationship, and each team member.

When Jean and I regrouped the next day, we shared how God had already begun to answer some of our prayers from the previous night. On this new day, we had been faced with more burdens, so we prayed over them again that night. More answered prayers greeted us the next day. We were in there over a week, and we counted up between seventy-five to 100 prayers the Lord had answered during our time there.

Oswald Chambers calls that sort of prayer *intercession*. In his book *My Utmost for His Highest,* he wrote,

> *If we are not heedful of the way the Spirit of God works in us, we will become spiritual hypocrites. We see where other folks are failing, and we turn our discern-*

ment into the gibe of criticism instead of into interces-
sion on their behalf. . . .

One of the subtlest burdens God ever puts on us as
saints is this burden of discernment concerning other
souls. He reveals things in order that we may take the
burden of these souls before Him and form the mind of
Christ about them, and as we intercede on His line, God
says He will give us "life for them that sin not unto
death." . . .[1]

If the Lord gives you the ability to see something that's not right or not honoring to the Lord, use that discernment for the purpose of prayer. If you have a gift of criticism, it may be that you have an inverted gift of discernment. If you keep the weight of that knowledge to yourself or tell it to other people, it won't do you any good. But if you use that same discernment and channel it into prayer, you will become a mighty prayer warrior. It has absolutely changed my prayer life to use my discernment for the purpose of prayer and not for the purpose of criticism.

Finally, we can **increase prayer's effectiveness through fasting**. When I was in a country closed to the gospel not long ago, I asked the Christians I visited to name some obstacles they were facing— some crooked and rough places that we could fast and pray over. One of those crooked places was in their public relations. The country's security is very tight. While I was there, people I knew were arrested and taken for interrogation. This kind of thing happens all the time.

---

1. Oswald Chambers, *My Utmost for His Highest* (1935; reprint, Westwood, N.J.: Barbour and Company, n.d.), p. 91.

So we began to fast and pray over the next days for the rough and crooked places in their public relations to be made smooth.

The day after the fast began, my friend and I visited a restaurant. I was taking pictures in the restaurant, and three people next to us were watching me take those pictures. I asked them if I could take their picture as well, and they huddled together and smiled for the camera.

Ten minutes after they left the restaurant, a vehicle drove up to the restaurant with one of those three people inside. She wanted to take me for a ride around the city and show me some of the sites. I was unable to join her, but when she left her card for me, I found out she was one of the administrators my friends had been struggling against for a long time in their public relations. Everyone was marveling that after one day of fasting and praying, we could make a connection like this that directly concerned their need.

So, there is something to fasting and praying that makes a difference to God. And it's something that God is bringing into our consciousness again. There are probably hundreds of thousands of people in churches all over the globe that are seeing God move through their fasts and prayers.

How about you? Do you have rough places and crooked places that need to be smoothed out? I would challenge you to write them down and begin to pray and fast over them. Is there something in your life that's really troubling you? Use that discernment for the purpose of prayer and not for the purpose of fault-finding. I promise that as you pray specifically, He will answer your prayers in His timing and in His way.

✦ Ney Bailey ✦

*I*nternational speaker and *Faith is Not a Feeling* author, Ney Bailey has served on Insight for Living's board of directors for more than twelve years. Ney travels the world on behalf of Campus Crusade for Christ, sharing Christ and helping people grow in their faith. Ney prays that upon reading her thoughts here, you would be encouraged to make prayer part of the fabric of your everyday life.

Fasting: Hungering for a Deeper Faith

"Blessed are those who hunger and thirst for righteousness, for they shall be satisfied."

(Matthew 5:6)

Fasting is a spiritual exercise of temporary self-denial to enhance our prayers and enrich our devotion to God. It's not a hunger strike or a way to earn points with God, or even a guarantee that God will answer our prayers the way we want Him to. Instead, fasting enhances our prayers by . . .

- Adding urgency and passion to our prayers
- Helping us set aside time for concentrated prayer
- Releasing spiritual power

Fasting also enriches our devotion to God by . . .

- Revealing the things that control us
- Helping us keep a balance
- Humbling us
- Focusing our thoughts on the Lord
- Opening our eyes to God's will
- Encouraging our dependence on God

"Fasting does not change God's hearing so much as it changes our praying." —Donald S. Whitney

KEEP A SOFT HEART: RESPONDING TO GOD IN FAITH

by Debbie Swindoll

Want to know how to live by faith in your everyday life? Learn a lesson from those who've gone before you to discover what it means to walk by faith.

My great Uncle Brian is an illusive figure from my childhood. I saw him only a couple of times while I was growing up. He spent the latter part of his life in a mental hospital, where he ultimately passed away. Although virtually absent from my childhood, Uncle Brian taught me something about faith that I will never forget.

Brian's son, Don, was killed in World War II, and the grief over Don's death sent Brian into a deep depression. Unable to shake his sorrow, Brian attended several tent meetings led by a traveling evangelist who had come to town. After responding to the altar call several evenings in a row yet finding no relief from his depression, the evangelist told my uncle he lacked sufficient faith to be healed. The disappointment and disillusionment of the tent meeting experience sent Brian into a tailspin from which he never recovered.

My uncle's experience illustrates how we often view faith—as some mysterious, dramatic force. Do we have enough faith to be healed of a chronic disease? To conquer a financial mountain? And if not, can we recover spiritually, or, like Brian, will we be derailed and defeated by a devastating life circumstance?

Certainly when we encounter large and unusual events, faith commands our trust. But that's not where we live on most days. What does faith look like amidst life's more mundane and usual situations? I don't know about you, but I'd rather learn from someone else's mistakes if they will help me avoid a few myself. The answer lies in Hebrews, but not in chapter 11, which is often referred to as the "Hall of Faith." Instead, let's look at Hebrews 3, which tells the tragic tale of a crisis of faith.

We could fill a textbook with the full and complete definition of faith, but let's begin with a very simple definition. Faith is *the action of a believing heart*. Read that again. Consider how you could put that definition in your own words.

Now, let's look at Hebrews 3:7–8:

> *Therefore, just as the Holy Spirit says,*
> *"Today if you hear His voice,*
> *Do not harden your hearts as when they provoked Me*
> *As in the day of trial in the wilderness . . ."*

The verse here, borrowed from Psalm 95, refers to the children of Israel's failure to go into the Promised Land after the spies had been sent to check it out. The story is told in Numbers 13 and 14.

It begins with a glorious exodus out of Egypt. Remember the drama? This event was filled with signs and wonders—the plagues in Egypt, the parting of the Red Sea, a pillar of cloud and fire, manna from heaven, and the building of a tabernacle that enabled God's glory to dwell among them. The nation of Israel then arrived on the edge of the Promised Land. But they wouldn't go in. They stood with their toes on the border of all God had promised to their father, Abraham, and they had a crisis of faith. God diagnosed their condition when He stated in 14:11, "How long will they not believe in Me?"

How did this happen? Through unbelief and disobedience, resulting in sin. They had heard the mixed report from the spies—though the land was flowing with milk and honey, it was inhabited by giants and the cities were fortified (13:27–33). They didn't *believe* God could and would deliver the land to them. So, in an act of disobedience, they refused to take their homeland (14:1–4). Despite all they had seen and experienced, they balked. Hebrews 4:2 explains that "the word they heard did not profit them, because it was not united by faith in those who heard." The end result? *Sin.*

> *Faith is the action of a believing heart—a heart that believes God's way is best and obeys His smallest urging amidst the most mundane day.*

This is where I typically become intoxicated with personal pride by thinking *I* would have reacted differently *if I* had been there. But Hebrews 3:12 sobers me with this caution: "Take care, brethren, that there not be in any one of you an evil, unbelieving heart that falls away from the living God."

How do we take care? How do we unite what we hear with faith? How do we prepare daily for those moments when we, too, will stand at a crossroads and hear God ask us to step among giants and trust Him that it will be okay?

The answer is quick to explain, but it takes a lifetime to live out. This phrase is repeated three times in Hebrews 3 and 4:

> "Today if you hear His voice, do not harden your hearts."
> (3:7–8, 15; 4:7)

While recently discussing this counsel with the ladies in my Bible study, I challenged them to ask God to magnify His voice to them for one day and to see how often they responded in obedience. (This is a gutsy prayer—right up there with praying for patience!) I was hoping this exercise would help us gauge how soft or hard our hearts were toward obeying God's Word.

I was not pleased with my personal results. I found it extremely easy to shush the voice cautioning me about my attitude or urging me to take a godly path in response to a difficult relationship. But ignoring that voice leads to a faithless life, like the children of Israel. If I ignored it, I would be on the same disobedient, unbelieving, and, ultimately, sinful path.

Let's return to our simple definition of faith: *Faith is the action of a believing heart*—a heart that *believes* God's way is best and obeys His smallest urging amidst the most mundane day. It's just like the author of Hebrews cautioned: "Today if you hear His voice, do not harden your heart."

I've thought about this very clear, straightforward exhortation from God's Word for quite a while now, and it had led me to three words of challenge. I urge you to act on them.

1. Pray that God would sensitize you to His voice. Spend time in His Word and ask the Holy Spirit to speak to you. Listen to that inner voice that urges you to act consistent with biblical truth and cautions you against words and deeds that fall short of a life motivated by love and grace.

2. Meditate on Hebrews 3:7–11. Read this passage several times. Mull it over in your mind as you go about your daily tasks. Ask God to reveal to you specific actions that harden your heart and distractions that lead you astray. Spend time in confession and get serious about dropping habits that steal your focus from Christ.

3. Renew your heart to obedience. Faith is built in the action of daily obedience. *Today* if you hear His voice, respond in faith by saying, "I believe you, Lord. Your way is best and I will walk in it—regardless."

What, then, is required of you in this life of faith? Is it somehow to screw up enough courage to trust some mysterious, dramatic force? Of course not. To keep trying harder to have *enough* faith so that maybe God would listen? No, it's not that either. We need not wait for a life-changing event or trust in a spiritual tent meeting to carry us through a personal crisis. The single moment when you chose to believe God and follow His prompting with obedient action is far less dramatic than you may have first thought.

Faith comes down to keeping a soft heart toward obeying God's Word. It means listening and being willing to respond when His Spirit prompts a change in your attitude or actions. You face that kind of opportunity every day of your life—in times of crisis and in times of routine.

The cumulative effect of a consistent and faithful obedience produces nothing short of a dramatically changed life. God uses changed lives to bring down strongholds and to face giants. May those lives be yours and mine.

Debbie Swindoll

*D*ebbie Swindoll is quietly putting her own name on the "Swindoll" brand. Daughter-in-law to Chuck Swindoll, Debbie has presented several series on the subject of faith to women's groups in church and retreat settings. She has often described the longest distance in life as the "12-18 inches from the head to the heart, but it is a journey everyone must make." She and her husband, Curt, are on that journey with three growing kids.

Waiting for Motherhood

Sarah bore her first and only son when she was ninety years old—Isaac, the son promised by the Lord. (Genesis 17:15–22; 21:1–7)

Rebekah's womb was barren, but when her husband, Isaac, prayed to the Lord, she conceived and gave birth to twins, Esau and Jacob. (Genesis 25:21–26)

Rachel was barren for many years before she conceived with Jacob's eleventh son, Joseph. She gave birth to one more son, Benjamin, before she died. (Genesis 29:31–30:24; 35:16–18)

Manoah's wife was barren until an angel of the Lord told her she would give birth to a Nazirite, whom she named Samson. He would deliver Israel from the Philistines if she refrained from wine and unclean foods while she was bearing him and did not bring a razor to his head while he lived. (Judges 13)

The Lord had closed Hannah's womb but reopened it when she vowed to offer her child to the Lord's service if He blessed her with a son. She called his name Samuel. (1 Samuel 1)

Elizabeth and her husband, Zacharias, were advanced in years and without children, but the Lord promised them a son who would prepare the way for the Lord. Elizabeth gave birth to John the Baptist. (Luke 1:1–25, 57–66)

FAITH THAT OVERCOMES OBSTACLES

by Sandra Glahn

What in your life looks impossible? Learn how to face life's most demanding circumstances with complete trust in God through one woman's step of faith.

My friend Valerie, a homemaker with four children, made an appointment to see her physician after experiencing dizzy spells. He ordered X-rays, and Valerie nearly passed out when she saw the pictures of the tumor in her brain. It was the size of an avocado.

Initially, everyone reeled from the shock. She and those around her wondered, What will happen to Randy and the kids? Is there a cure? Will there be another Christmas together?

As she tells it, when she began to yell at her kids or grow irritable with her husband, she excused it by telling herself, "I have brain cancer. What does God expect?"

What *does* God expect? As a follower of Christ, Val wants to magnify the Lord in this trial. So she approached Him with one key question: "What do You expect of me?" While her cancer makes it more difficult to do right, she has found that the same principle applies in sickness and health: To receive God's commendation when facing a seemingly impossible situation, we have to exercise *faith*.

What in your life looks impossible? Maybe you or someone you love faces something as serious as brain cancer. Or perhaps it's the knowledge that unless God does a miracle, your marriage won't last another year. Or maybe you toy with a secret habit that—if you don't get a grip on it—will destroy you. Each of us faces some overwhelming obstacle because we're all broken, needy people. And lots of people through history have asked the same question Valerie asked: "When I face such a situation, what does God expect?"

One person in particular stands out. She lived in Jesus' time, and we know her as the woman with the issue of blood. We find her story in Mark 5:25–34, and in it we see three demonstrations of biblical faith.

First of all, *faith takes us to Christ when we're at the end of ourselves.* This woman had endured bleeding for twelve years. The text says she had a "flow" of blood (v. 29), and it's the same word other ancient writers used to refer to menstrual bleeding. According to the Law, everywhere she sat became unclean. Everything she touched became ceremonially defiled. She had to remove herself from participation in the faith community because God required that those with emissions disassociate themselves from community worship. This woman had been a social outcast for more than a decade.

What caused her malady? While some translations say she was hemorrhaging, a gynecologist I consulted said she'd have bled to death long before if that had been the case. He listed a number of conditions that might cause long-term bleeding, one possibility being uterine cancer. A woman who's had uterine cancer for twelve years, assuming it has metastasized, would be in intense pain and near death. If that was true, the woman had not only been rejected as a social outcast, but she had also endured excruciating physical pain.

We also know that she spent all she had in the hands of doctors (v. 26). Nothing she tried had helped; the text tells us that instead of getting better, she grew worse. So she was at the end of herself when she came to Jesus.

What about you? Have you come to Him and acknowledged your need? Faith takes us to Christ with a clear understanding that we're out of resources and have no other options left.

This woman also shows us that *faith drives us to trust in Christ.* She inconspicuously touched His garment— probably His prayer tassels—because she believed He could heal (v. 28). This woman's faith involved more than

> Faith takes us to Christ with a clear understanding that we're out of resources and have no other options left.

mental assent. So sure was she in her belief that it drove her to action. She pursued Jesus, pushing her way through a mass of people who had probably long known her as a defiled woman.

Jesus certainly did the seemingly impossible for this woman. The text says that when she stretched out her hand, "immediately the flow of her blood was dried up; and she felt in her body that she was healed of her affliction" (v. 29). If this woman had uterine cancer, her body would have been racked by intense pain. And perhaps in that moment, all her disease-related discomfort ceased. She knew instantly that Jesus had healed her.

God can accomplish the impossible in us as well. One woman from my church has a brother who rebelled so openly that she told the pastor, "Even God couldn't change *his* heart." Today that brother is a youth pastor. God specializes in doing the impossible. Do you really believe Christ can help you? And does that belief drive you to pursue Him—to draw on His strength as you face insurmountable odds? He is worthy of your trust.

What was the Lord's response to the woman's reaching out? He realized that power had gone out from Him (v. 30). That doesn't mean she drained Him of power; it means He felt power proceed from Him, perhaps in the same way you or I feel power proceed from us when we hit a softball. Having felt that, He kept looking to see who had done it. He wanted to know, "Who touched Me?" (v. 30).

This was not what the woman had hoped for—she had hoped to remain anonymous. And her next action teaches us a third truth about faith: *Faith responds to Christ in obedience, even when He calls us to do a hard thing.* Mark noted, "The woman, fearing and trembling, aware of what had happened to her, came and fell down before Him and told him the whole truth" (v. 33).

Just imagine. She was terrified. She dreaded being singled out. But Jesus was looking for her, so she came and fell at His feet. We read about people falling at the Lord's feet in Scripture, and it's easy to think this was an everyday occurrence back then. But it wasn't. It was more like a once-in-a-lifetime deal.

Have you ever fallen at someone's feet? I did once—when I was thirteen. My boyfriend broke up with me, and I thought my life was over. So I grabbed his feet and begged him not to leave me. It was an act of utter and humble desperation. (OK, and stupidity too.) When you fall at someone's feet, your body language says your life is over— if not physically, at least emotionally—unless the person who has the power to intervene does something. And that is the stance this woman took.

Then she told all. Everything. How humiliating, to talk about menstrual problems in front of a huge crowd! But that is what the Lord asked of her. He expected her to give testimony to His goodness, to share the PG-13–rated story when she doubtless wished her life had been rated G. And she obeyed.

Now, what happened next should inspire us. Simply put, Jesus said to her, "Daughter!" (v. 34). Why is this significant? Because it's the only time in the entire New Testament where we read that He called *anyone* a daughter. And lest the reader doubt just how precious a daughter is, Mark continued in the next section to talk about Jairus' daughter, who had died but whom Jesus would raise from death (vv. 35–43). She was the beloved daughter of a father in anguish. "Daughter!" Do you long for that kind of affirmation? He longs to give it to you.

Jesus went on to tell the woman, "Your faith has made you well; go in peace and be healed of your affliction" (v. 34). Not only did He affirm her faith, but He also sent her home healed. And while physical healing came instantly, social and emotional healing had only begun.

In Hebrews 11:6, we read that without faith it is impossible to please God but that He rewards those who diligently seek Him. Our faith can bring that same glorious commendation—"Daughter!"—when we act on what we beleive.

Valerie is developing that kind of faith in her daily fight against brain cancer. Yes, she experiences anguish, and no one's pretending it's easy. But through her disease she has also gained an eternal perspective that makes people want to sit at her feet to catch the overflow as she shares about Christ. She has set her focus on something even more important to her than celebrating another Christmas with her family, as important as that is. She desires more than anything to be a woman of faith, to become the kind of child to whom a loving, heavenly Father can freely say, "Well done, Daughter!"

Sandra Glahn

Sandra Glahn is a freelance writer and is editor of *Kindred Spirit*, the magazine of Dallas Theological Seminary. Sandra is also a sought-after speaker on the topic of infertility. "Throughout a decade-long journey through infertility and pregnancy loss that led finally to the adoption of a much-desired daughter," Sandra said, "this biblical account was the one that most encouraged me."

All praise to the God and Father of our Master, Jesus the Messiah! Father of all mercy! God of all healing counsel! *He comes alongside us when we go through hard times,* and before you know it, He brings us alongside someone else who is going through hard times so that we can be there for that person just as God was there for us. We have plenty of hard times that come from following the Messiah, but no more so than the good times of His healing comfort—we get a full measure of that, too.

2 Corinthians 1:3–4 (THE MESSAGE)

PRIORITIES: PURSUING WHAT MATTERS MOST

by Dr. Cheryl Fawcett

*Do you need more time or do you need more focus?
Discover how to invest the next twenty-four hours for
eternity's gain.*

Stressed out was what I was. Way too much to do. Way too little time to do it. I hurried here and there, trying to be more efficient. I studied time management to streamline the comings and goings of my daily activities. Still, it seemed like the most important things in my life were constantly postponed for later, another time, a more convenient time slot that never seemed to come.

I prayed for more hours in my day, but I finally realized that I had already been given enough hours in each day to do the will of God. What I needed was a way to determine God's priorities for my life. I didn't need more time, I needed focus—the ability to pursue what mattered most. I desired the freedom to leave other, less important but do-able tasks undone.

I ruminated on Jesus' life pace as recorded in the Gospels. He didn't run from place to place like a frantic, overworked slave. He lived His life deliberately. He accomplished the important without being tyrannized by the urgent. At times, He walked away from a sincere, legitimate invitation for assistance and moved on to another town or assignment with the confidence that He was accomplishing what mattered most to His Father. I needed that prioritized focus in my life. Perhaps you have felt this same desire.

So, what does matter most? What are God's highest priorities for your life? This well-worn principle offers you guidance: Only two things on this earth last forever—the Word of God and people. You can't take a U-Haul of accomplishments to heaven, but you can take other people that you introduce to Christ and, with them, enjoy eternity praising our Maker. But with so many people and so many needs, how do you know which ones to respond to and which ones to pass on by?

This checklist of musings can guide your reflection:

✓ How do I know my own priorities?

✓ What do I talk about most?

✓ What do I spend the most money on?

✓ What do I spend my time doing?

✓ What do I worry about?

✓ What fills the quiet moments of my thoughts and dreams?

Your real priorities can be revealed by a careful look at your checkbook, your day planner, your to-do list, and your diary entries.

Think about your priorities. Ask your friends what they hear from you most often. Check with your mate to find out what he believes to be your life goals. Ask a coworker where you focus your conversations. Ask your children what they think is important to you. The answers might be painful, but those around us have 20/20 perspective, while we often have shortsightedness or tunnel vision.

Jesus gave some startling and valuable insight on priorities in His mountainside conversation with the disciples. Matthew 6:19–24 records three challenges that could ultimately help focus your priorities.

The first challenge, outlined in verses 19–21, describes the *location* of your treasures — are they earthly or heavenly? Are you constantly talking about the stock market's ups and downs? Is your focus on the rising gas and electric rates? Are you consumed with making money to buy the latest time-saving device to simplify your life? Do you stay up late at night, planning how you can get that job promotion? If so, then your treasures are vulnerable to inflation, theft, or loss because they are stored in an earthly vault.

Placing your treasures out of this world will greatly impact your priorities.

Are you planning ways that you can give more to your church's missions outreach project? Do you see your child's sports event as a way to talk with other parents about their lives and challenges?

Are you talking with your neighbor who needs Christ while building a genuine friendship to help that happen? Are you using your skills and talents in your church's children's or youth ministry so that you get heaven's applause? Placing your treasures out of this world will greatly impact your priorities. So, where is your focus—heaven or earth?

The second challenge found in verses 22–23, reflects the *object* of your focus—are you focused on the good or the greed? When you focus on the good, you are consumed with the good of others. When you focus on the greed, your whole life takes on a self-centered approach. Followers of Christ spend their time, energy, money, efforts, and dreams on accomplishing good for others. They have no time for the evil pursuits of this world. They do more than stop running after the bad; they actively strive for the good, the noble, the excellent. So, what is the object of your focus—the good or the greed?

The third challenge in verse 24 asks about your *owner*—do you serve God or money? It may be possible to have more than one employer, but you can only have one master. A slave offers total devotion and complete focus to his master. He doesn't report for work each morning and then decide if the master's plans suit his personal preferences. He reports for and is committed to doing whatever the master decides. The slave doesn't vote on the tasks; he just does them. You cannot give your all to more than one owner. You will cheat one or the other or, more likely, both in your effort to juggle dual allegiance. Lest we misunderstand, Jesus named the masters. It is quite interesting that He didn't say God or Satan but rather God or money. We will either be driven to provide for ourselves or to allow God to provide for us.

God's priority for the single person is that they serve Him with a whole heart (1 Corinthians 7:32–35). God's priority for the married person is that they meet the needs of their partner (Ephesians 5:22–30). God's priority for married couples with children is that they bring them up in the nurture and admonition of the Lord, training them to love and serve God (Ephesians 6:4). For every believer, God's priorities are to love Him first and to love our neighbors as we love ourselves.

Every day you are challenged with how to invest the twenty-four hours the Master provides for you. Let's determine to store our treasures in the next life, focus on the good, and serve the agenda of our Owner. When we do, our choices come into clearer focus. Many of the good things that we could do we don't have time to do because our lives will be consumed with the *eternal*, the *good*, and the *Master's agenda!*

Dr. Cheryl Fawcett

*D*r. Cheryl Fawcett serves as associate professor of Christian Education at Christian Heritage College in El Cajon, California. She says, "Overload was a way of life that I resented but didn't know how to change. These thoughts are drawn from how God has directed my life and thoughts toward godly change."

And She Shall Be Called . . .

Biblical Women's Names and Their Meanings

Abigail—*cause of joy*
Abishag—*my father wanders*
Ahlai—*O would that!*
Anna—*grace*
Atarah—*crown*

Bashemath—*perfumed*
Bernice—*victorious*

Candace—*queen*
Chloe—*green herb*

Deborah—*bee*
Delilah—*delicate*
Dinah—*justice*
Dorcas—*gazelle*
Drusilla—*watered by the dew*

Elizabeth—*a worshipper of God*
Esther—*a star*
Eunice—*conquering well*
Euodias—*prosperous journey*
Eve—*life*

Gomer—*completion*

Hadassah—*myrtle*
Hannah—*gracious*
Hephzibah—*my delight is in her*
Hodesh—*new moon*

Iscah—*she will look out*

Jael—*gazelle*
Jedidah—*Jehovah's darling*
Jemima—*little dove*
Jerusah—*married*
Joanna—*the Lord is grace*
Jochebed—*Jehovah's glory*
Judith—*the praised one*
Julia—*curly headed*

Keren-happuch—*beautifier*

Leah—*wearied*
Lydia—*bending*

Mara—*bitter*
Martha—*mistress of the house*
Mary—*bitterness*

Mehetabel—*benefited of God*
Michal—*who is like Jehovah?*
Milcah—*counsel*

Naamah—*sweetness*
Narah—*child of the Lord*
Naomi—*my joy*

Orpah—*a fawn*

Peninnah—*coral*
Persis—*one who takes by storm*
Phebe—*pure*
Priscilla—*worthy*

Rachel—*ewe*
Rebecca—*captivating*
Rhoda—*rose*
Ruth—*something worth seeing*

Salome—*peace*
Sapphira—*sapphire*
Sarah—*princess*
Shua—*rich*
Susanna—*a white lily*
Syntyche—*fortunate*

Tabitha—*gazelle*
Tamar—*a palm tree*
Taphath—*a drop of myrrh*
Timna—*restraint*
Tirzah—*pleasantness*
Tryphena—*dainty one*

Vashti—*beautiful woman*

Zeresh—*gold*
Zillah—*protection*
Zipporah—*little bird*

TRUSTING GOD IN SICKNESS AND IN HEALTH

by Dr. Cheryl Fawcett

Illness is not an enemy—it's the tool God uses to shape, refine, and mold you to the character of His Son.

"Your cancer has returned. I'm sorry." My surgeon had hoped for the best but was obliged to report the worst. Survivors are those that make it five years without a recurrence, but only four years had passed since my first battle with cancer. I had been close, but now I was so very far away again. I was immediately immersed into the world of white lab coats again, with the blood tests, CAT scans, bone scans, chemotherapy, radiation, nausea, fatigue, unwanted time off, and isolation that comes with it.

It had been a much longer haul than four years, for prior to cancer I battled severe back pain for over thirteen years, enduring two debilitating spinal fusions. I was so tired of being sick, so weary of vainly searching for medical and spiritual relief.

Once the emotional and physical numbness began to wear off, questions flooded my mind and heart. *Why me? Why this again? Don't you have someone else that you could pick on for a while, Lord? I am trying to serve you. I am doing my best to use every ounce of strength to aid your cause. I thought I had learned the lessons from cancer. Aren't you satisfied? Do you intend to take my life?* My attitude was temporarily out of control.

Peace—that's what I needed. Perspective was what I longed for. Grace to sustain me was my plea. Hope was in desperately low supply. I knew that I was secure for eternity, but surviving the nasty here and now was a different matter. I had peace *with* God but not the peace *of* God as I faced yet another severe health challenge.

I knew that I was standing in grace, the kind of established, abiding, continuing grace that marks the life of a faithful follower of Christ. And as Paul said in Romans 5:2, I was "[rejoicing] in the hope of the glory of God" (NIV). While that hope was a certain reality, it was also a future event. Hopelessness became my immediate, dominant reality.

The next paragraph of Paul's letter, Romans 5:1–4, provides critical insight into how to handle crippling, crushing tribulations—health related or otherwise. Paul talks about rejoicing in the face of pressures and troubles. This joy doesn't come in one easy pill but rather in three installments of patience, experience, and finally, hope!

There were many times during the cancer trial that I wondered if I would ever have hope again. At one point, I determined to end the treatment and let the cancer take its course in my body. I was too tired to continue fighting off the effects of the chemotherapy. I needed Paul's reminder that the troubles in our lives are working for us, that they are God's messengers to accomplish something of significance (Romans 8:28). The trial is not an end in itself but a means to godliness when we allow God to accomplish His work in us.

I had prayed for relief up to that point. I wanted the trouble out of my life. I wanted to be free of the struggle.

God had other plans. He wanted to develop *patience* in my life. I knew about the grit-your-teeth-and-press-on-in-your-own-strength kind of endurance. I was a veteran of the pull-yourself-up-by-your-own-spiritual-bootstraps mentality. But God was working on something else—a cheerful, hopeful endurance. I knew nothing of that variety. God wanted me to remain under the tribulation. He taught me to bear up under the load rather than dump it entirely.

What I discovered was that even though my physical condition held a greater degree of gravity the second time around, I was not nearly as panicked, frantic, or restless as before. Despite the greater magnitude of trouble, God revealed that the trouble had indeed worked a good deal of patience in me. Step one—partially accomplished!

> Joy doesn't come in one easy pill but rather in three installments of patience, experience, and finally, hope!

Patience under the trial is the platform from which God begins to develop His next stepping-stone toward hope: *experience*. Some translations use the word *character*. It shows a trustful confidence, a proof of passing the test, a determination to be acceptable. God encouraged me with a deepening prayer relationship. I went from merely *saying* prayers to *breathing* prayers: "God, give me enough strength to get to the couch. God, I love you today. God, help me as I dress. God, give me the determination to drive to work with Your help. God, help me climb the three flights of stairs to my office. God, help me gather my teaching materials for today's session. God, I need You this moment, and the next, and the next . . ." As I leaned on Him and more willingly remained under the trial, He refined my character a little at a time.

Others around me began to notice and point out evidence of that character in my life that I hadn't even observed. How sweet were their affirmations of God's refining work in my life: "You are so strong in spirit. . . . You seem to find your strength in God. . . . You give me courage to face the struggle in my life with God's help." I had thought cancer was my enemy, but now I realized God was using it as a tool to shape, refine, and mold me. Paul declared that experience produces *hope*. Hope is that expectation, even confidence, that God is producing Christ in us. Indeed, God was giving me hope—not just in the future, but in the here and now!

Learning the right attitude in times of trouble may be difficult, but it is more challenging in times of renewed health. Do I need God, I had to ask myself, now that my strength has returned? Do I remember His goodness and grace and thank Him often, now that I don't need to cry out for every breath and every moment? Have I taken on the "I'll-take-it-from-here" attitude? While difficult times introduce dependence, times of ease can refine it.

Moses warned the people in Deuteronomy 6:10–19 that when they came into a land that had been promised them, a land overflowing with the resources that they lacked in the wilderness, they were to be careful *not* to forget the Lord. Obviously, forgetting God when circumstances are going the right way is a natural but wrong thing to do. Israel needed to continue fearing the Lord and serving Him exclusively, and so must we.

By God's grace, my health has stabilized over the past year and a half. I've been free from life-threatening infections. Gone is the debilitating tiredness that resulted from intense doses of chemotherapy and radiation. Left behind are the moments, hours, and days of isolation. It is my desire to retain a deep, noticeable patience and the experience and hope that God worked in my life through those challenging days.

I've learned that when we're stuck asking *why*, we may miss the more important matter of *what* the Master wants to perfect in us through our sicknesses or times of health. It is common to struggle with doubt, but to camp in that plain of desperation is a dead end. God has turned my journey into a pursuit of reliance on Him and hope for His ultimate glory.

⇒ Dr. Cheryl Fawcett ⇐

*H*aving struggled with fifteen years of back pain, two rounds with cancer with chemo and daily radiation, 15 surgical procedures, and three life threatening infections, Dr. Cheryl Fawcett has watched God develop hope in her life despite the trials. Cheryl is Associate Professor of Christian Education at Christian Heritage College, El Cajon, CA.

Private Ministries of Women in the Bible

Moses' mother nursed and cared for him yet made no claim to him after he had been adopted by Pharoah's daughter. **Exodus 2:8–10**

Rahab hid and helped two Hebrews escape Jericho as they spied out the land. **Joshua 2**

An unnamed woman killed the wicked king, Abimelech, by dropping a millstone on his head. **Judges 9:53**

Ruth was valued as more precious than seven sons to Naomi because of her faithfulness. **Ruth 4:13–15**

Hannah gives Samuel to God, to serve in the temple, as she had promised she would if God gave her a son. **1 Samuel 1:26-28**

A nameless woman hides Jonathan down a well when Absalom hunted and wanted to kill him. **2 Samuel 17:19**

A nameless, "wise" woman interceded for her city when Joab attacked her city. She yelled over the wall that she wanted to talk with Joab, eventually saving her city from destruction. **2 Samuel 20**

Private Ministries of Women in the Bible

The widow at Zarephath provided food for Elijah in a time of drought. **1 Kings 17**

❧ ~ ❧

A well-to-do woman from Shunamem often gave Elisha room and board in her home. **2 Kings 4:8**

❧ ~ ❧

Unnamed servant girl who tells Nahaam, her master about Elijah's healing power, **2 Kings 5**

❧ ~ ❧

You would think Esther, as a queen, would be considered to have had a public ministry, however, everything Esther did on behalf of God's people was private, under the secrecy of certain death should she have been discovered. **The book of Esther**

❧ ~ ❧

Faithful prayer warrior Anna never left the temple but worshiped night and day, fasting and praying, waiting for the redemption of Israel. When she was eighty-four, she saw the answer to her prayer in Jesus, when Mary and Joseph presented Him in the temple. **Luke 2:36**

❧ ~ ❧

From the time we first meet Mary, Jesus' mother in **Luke 2**, she responded in faith and willing obedience to whatever God required of her. We're told she pondered all the mystery and miracle in her heart.

A QUIET PRESENCE

by Sandra L. Glahn

Offering comfort can be as much about what you don't say as what you do.

I ran to the grocery store to pick up steaks. Passing through the floral section, I impulsively grabbed a bouquet of roses, anticipating the most memorable dinner of my life. After three years of infertility treatment, I could finally announce to my husband Gary that he would have a new name—Dad.

We revealed our secret to our delighted families. "Finally!" everyone squealed. And we began anticipating how our lives would change.

But early one morning, I felt pain and knew something was wrong. For the next twenty-four hours we waited for test results, pleading with God to spare our child's life. By the next evening, a miscarriage had crushed our dreams. Repeatedly in the hours that followed, Gary wrapped his arms around my shaking shoulders and rested his cheek against mine as I choked back sobs.

That was eleven years ago. As the years passed, this scene repeated itself in our home many times. The only difference was that with each loss, our unbridled sense of optimism turned into caution and emotional distancing.

The wait for our daughter Alexandra (who joined our family in 1995 through the miracle of adoption) spanned a decade that included years of invasive medical treatment, multiple miscarriages, and three failed adoptions.

I always hesitate to tell my story because I don't like to engage in the Suffering Olympics—going for the gold in competing over who has hurt the most. We've had some pain in our lives, but most people have endured worse. Nevertheless, during our decade of struggle, I began to take note of what did and didn't help when others offered words or gestures of comfort. I still make mistakes as I try to help those in pain, but here are a few things I've picked up along the way.

First, be silent, and listen. Our quiet presence is often the greatest comfort. Dr. Bill Cutrer, an obstetrician who is now a pastor, shares how during his first year of medical practice, he sat with a couple who lost a baby at twenty-three weeks. Feeling at a total loss for words, he sat in silence and wept with them: "I felt surprised when they later thanked me profusely saying, 'You said just the right words.'"

What words? I wondered.

Precisely. "The deepest feeling always shows itself in silence; not in silence, but restraint," wrote poet Marianne Moore more than a century ago. Her words still ring true today.

Silence keeps us from asking nosey questions or saying, "You'll get over it," "Time heals all wounds," or "At least . . ." Other unhelpful statements include, "It must be God's will," "I know exactly how you feel," or any statement starting with "Maybe God . . ."

A pastor who suffered multiple losses over a period of six months said, "The most significant thing I learned was that the high-sounding, though true, theological axioms sound so trite, and are immensely irritating. Either God brings those thoughts to your mind with His comfort, or they seem of little help." Job's friends did well for the first week when they sat and said nothing. They got into trouble only after they opened their mouths.

Often our "ministry of presence," just showing up, is all that's needed. However, we must balance this with the "ministry of absence." After his wife's hospitalization, one husband said, "People should plan to leave quickly from all visits. Give the patient a chance to say, 'No, please stay,' instead of thinking, 'I wish this person would leave.'" We must let those who are grieving be the ones to decide who stays, how long they stay, and whether to remain silent or talk. They may long for company. Yet they may also wish for time alone without anyone scrutinizing their actions or words.

> *At times, we must also recognize that the family of God can minister some comfort, but in times of deepest loss, the only One who can truly console is the God of the family.*

If you speak, keep it simple. Note that only one of these is longer than five words: "I'm sorry." "I'm here if you want to talk." "I feel sad for you." "How are you doing?" "May I hug you?" "It's okay to cry." "I love you."

Also, touch them. Depending on the closeness of the relationship, take your friend's hand when you tell her you're sorry, or give her a warm handshake, a pat on the back, a shoulder hug, or a bear hug. If in doubt, simply ask, "May I hug you?" Martin Luther wrote, "We are all little Christs—when we touch, He touches."

Next, weep with those who weep (Romans 12:15). Notice that the apostle Paul, when writing this admonition, did not say, "Tell stories to those who weep," ("I know someone who had that surgery and she . . ."). Nor does he say to instruct, share a verse with, cheer up, or even be strong for those who weep.

"Those who cry with me provide the greatest relief," I wrote in my journal during one of our losses. "With them I feel free to express emotion, so my tears can flow freely." When a friend's father died, he told me, "Weeping needs an echo." Shared weeping shows others that we love them enough to let their pain wound us. It also assures them that they aren't foolish for "getting so emotional."

By accepting their honest feelings we can show hurting people we care. This goes beyond "allowing them to cry." The more difficult part for many of us may be letting them vent anger. Anger in its various forms is part of the grief process. It can range from irritability to loud outbursts.

God filled His Word with stories about people of faith who questioned or got angry when life was difficult. Moses wondered why God was so hard on him, requesting, "If this is how you are going to treat me, put me to death right now—if I have found favor in your eyes—and do not let me face my own ruin" (Numbers 11:15 NIV). Once

Moses expressed himself, God came to his aid and met his need. We must trust Him to do the same for those we love.

Next, let them know that their mourning is justified. Statements such as "That must be hard," or "That's terrible," are far better than, "It's not so bad," or "How can you feel that way?" When my uncle died suddenly, the most comforting thing anyone said to me was, "That stinks. That really stinks."

And don't forget to pray. This may seem obvious, yet a *U.S. News and World Report* poll revealed that the average believer spends less than two minutes in prayer daily. The average pastor fares little better. Apparently, we believe in prayer, but we fail to pray. We must ask for God's wisdom to guide us through the mine fields of others' volatile feelings. And we must also recognize that the family of God can minister some comfort, but in times of deepest loss, the only One who can truly console is the God of the family.

Also, if anyone is going to offer spiritual encouragement, let it be the hurting person. When someone having a great day says "Trust God" to someone in pain, it sounds like a heartless accusation. It also robs the suffering believer of the opportunity to testify about God's grace. It's the comforter's job to weep; it's the hurting person's job, when he or she is ready, to share about God's sufficiency. Too often it happens the other way around. Would-be comforters leave people weeping after "bearing witness" to them that God is sufficient.

"God allows bad to happen, but makes good from it," wrote Patti, who has endured two rapes. "It took me a long time to conclude that I'm not going to know why it happened, but ultimately God's love and power are greater than those men." Patti's statement about God's character has greater impact because the person uttering it has been in the fire.

Another important way to express compassion is through initiating. It's nearly impossible for the person in pain to find energy to initiate. If you want to help, don't say "Call me if you need anything." Instead, make a specific offer: "What groceries can I pick up for you?" "Could I mow your lawn?" or "May I bring dinner tonight?" (Be sure to ask for preferences in food and time of delivery. Disposable pans help too.) After my first miscarriage, a friend from church baked us a chocolate cake. "I didn't want to send a plant or plaque which might later remind you of your loss," he told us.

Even if you hardly know them, go ahead and send a card, flowers, or tickets for a night out. One grieving man wrote, "I appreciated e-mail. I could read it when I felt like it and react freely. It's okay to yell at your computer."

Caring for others takes energy, effort, and patience. Days may turn to months and even years, making it seem that the pain will never end. But "suffer long" with them.

Two weeks after her son drowned, Amanda wept openly. She told a friend, "Already people act like they think I should be getting over it."

"I was talking with a friend who lost her husband less than a year ago," says author Madeleine L'Engle. "I told her, 'I miss my husband just as much today.' She said, 'I'm not sure I like that.' I said, 'Yes, you do. You don't want to stop missing him.'"

Finally, a note of caution: Never use others' pain to gain something for yourself, not even a good feeling about reaching out.

People facing significant losses are often thrown into the arena of attention. If you are called upon to help, **keep your observations to yourself,** being careful never to use the information you've gained to prove you're "in the know."

Sometimes it's easy to use others' pain to demonstrate subtly how great we are, like sweeping into a meeting and announcing, "Sorry I'm late; I was counseling someone who had a marital crisis," rather than quietly slipping into our seats. We must pray for the humility never to use anyone else's need as a workshop, as Dr. Eugene Peterson puts it, "to cobble together makeshift, messianic work that inflates our importance and indispensability."

Though we may want desperately to take the pain away, we know we can't. However, in a variety of ways, we can assure people through our actions that God loves them and we do, too. The job requires only a few simple pieces of equipment: two ears, feet that initiate, silent tongues, tear ducts, tender eyes, soft shoulders, and loving arms.

Sandra Glahn

Sandra Glahn says, "I like to think of providing comfort as being a lot like the Special Olympics—regardless of our own weaknesses, we all help each other make it to the finish line. I owe a lot to my own cheerleaders." Sandra, a recent graduate of Dallas Theological Seminary, is a freelance writer and is editor of DTS's *Kindred Spirit* magazine.

A Closing Prayer from Chuck

Our Father, I thank You today for women of strength and dignity. Thank You for their roles of responsibility, which, it seems, never end. Thank You for their calling, as clear a calling as any man or woman has ever had into ministry. Thank You for their families. Use what has been said in this book to reassure them of their significance in Your eyes and their importance in their family's eyes.

Strengthen them with purpose and vision for the life you've called them to. Guard them from chasing shadows and clinging to broken dreams. Enrich their faith with keen insight into Your Word and a heart for applying Your truth on the practical platform of daily living. May we learn from them consistently. And may they learn from You humbly.

In the name of Jesus Christ, who loved us and gave Himself for us, we pray. *Amen.*

ADDITIONAL RESOURCES FROM INSIGHT FOR LIVING

How else can you help me grow in my understanding of the Christian life?

If you want to grow, Insight for Living wants to help you—whether you've recently trusted Christ as your Savior or have walked with Him for years. Our goal is to help you gain new insights into the Bible through a variety of resources:

✔ An encouraging **monthly letter from Chuck Swindoll**

✔ An instructional, thought-provoking **monthly newsletter**

✔ More than 100 different **Bible-teaching audiocassette series** to encourage you toward godly living. Subjects range from Bible book studies and Bible character portraits to topical surveys—all from Chuck's reliable, applicable, and enjoyable teaching ministry.

✔ **Bible study guides** that correspond with every audiocassette series for your personal or group study

✔ **Pastoral counseling by mail** for trustworthy spiritual answers about life's difficult questions

✔ **Christian books you can trust** for spiritual growth, character building, and doctrinal authenticity

Call or write for more information about any of these resources. We'd love to help you find the resources that best fit your needs— and we're looking forward to hearing from you.

www.insight.org

United States
Insight for Living • Post Office Box 269000 • Plano, Texas 75026-9000
Toll-free 1-800-772-8888, 24 hours a day, 7 days a week

International locations, call (972) 796-1200,
8:00 A.M. to 4:30 P.M., Pacific time, Monday through Friday

Canada
Insight for Living Ministries • Post Office Box 2510
Vancouver, BC V6B 3W7
Toll-free 1-800-663-7639, 24 hours a day, 7 days a week

Australia and the South Pacific
Insight for Living, Inc. • 20 Albert Street
Blackburn, VIC 3130, Australia
Toll-free 1800 772 888 or (03) 9877-4277
8:30 A.M. to 5:00 P.M., Monday through Friday